More Hold'em Wisdom
for All Players

More Hold'em Wisdom
for All Players

by Daniel Negreanu

Cardoza Publishing

Cardoza Publishing is the foremost gaming and gambling publisher in the world with a library of almost 200 up-to-date and easy-to-read books and strategies. These authoritative works are written by the top experts in their fields and with more than 10 million books in print, represent the best-selling and most popular gaming books anywhere.

2016 Fourth Printing
Copyright ©2008 by Daniel Negreanu
- All Rights Reserved -

This material is printed by special arrangement with Card Shark Media
World Poker Tour cover photo courtesy of WPT Enterprises, Inc.
© 2005 WPT Enterprises, Inc.
- All Rights Reserved -

Library of Congress Catalog Card No: 2006922958
ISBN: 1-58042-210-1   ISBN 13: 978-158042-210-9

Visit our new web site (www.cardozabooks.com) or write us for a full list of books, advanced and computer strategies.

CARDOZA PUBLISHING
P.O. Box 98115, Las Vegas, NV 89193
Toll Free Phone (800)577-WINS
email: cardozabooks@aol.com
www.cardozabooks.com

DANIEL

Kid Poker

Daniel Negreanu, one of the most popular and charismatic players in poker, exudes the confidence of a new generation of poker players raised on video games, the Internet and MTV. Best known for both his aggressive style of play and his amiable personality, Daniel has cashed in for millions and millions of dollars. He is the leading money-winner in the World Poker Tour (WPT), and until the recent dramatic surge in World Series of Poker (WSOP) prize money, he was the all-time money winner in poker tournament history.

Negreanu's accomplishments include four WSOP bracelets, two WPT championships, Player-of-the-Year awards in both the WPT and WSOP, more than 40 wins in tournaments worldwide, and international stardom as one of the best tournament players in the world.

Negreanu is the author of two other books, the new "bible" of hold'em poker, *Daniel Negreanu's Power Hold'em Strategy*, and the companion book to this one, *Hold'em Wisdom for All Players*. He is also an esteemed contributor to Doyle Brunson's *Super System 2*, the author of a nationally syndicated newspaper column, "Playing Poker with Daniel Negreanu," and a spokesman for pokerstars.com. Daniel is one of the creators and stars of PokerVT.com, a new web-based virtual training system that simulates one-on-one poker instruction and in-depth video-based analysis.

CONTENTS

INTRODUCTION

You're holding a book that can take your hold'em game to the next level. I've built on the 50 concepts and strategies I covered the first time around in *Hold'em Wisdom for All Players* with 50 new and powerful tips.

The 50 easy-to-read lessons in this book are divided into four parts to quickly get you on the path to consistent profits in cash games and to the final table in tournaments.

I started off with some of my most effective tournament strategies, targeting a particular winning concept with each piece. The second part of this book shows you how to identify and play against different types of players and how to take advantage of position to rake in more pots. The third section shows you the advanced no-limit hold'em betting strategies being used today by the pros. You'll also learn how to use the small-ball approach to save you from disaster when you're beaten and to lead you to the biggest possible win when you've got the best hand—or at least when your opponent thinks you do!

Wrapping it all up, in the last section, I take you into the think tank and show you how to turn your poker wisdom into profits. Together, we progress through the thought processes that pros use to make quality decisions to come up with the best play.

If you love playing poker as much as I do, you owe it to yourself to explore new ideas, learn more ways to polish your skills, and get the most enjoyment possible from playing poker. I hope this book leads to greater enjoyment of hold'em and, best of all, more chips!

PART I:
WINNING TOURNAMENTS WITH SMART PLAY

Winning a no-limit hold'em tournament is one of the premier highs you will ever experience in your poker career. I still remember the rush I got when I won my first tournament, even though I didn't win very much money. Now that tournament poker has become a national pastime and is broadcast in prime time, the prize pools range from big to humongous. Just about every poker player I know wants to win a WPT title or a WSOP bracelet. But like anything else, you can't win it if you're not in it. Here are some of my top tips for getting there in tournaments.

1

Five Secrets to Success in Major Poker Tournaments

If you're saving up your money to play in one of the big $10,000 events on the poker circuit, these five tips will help make you a winner.

1. Don't lay odds on your preflop raises

Let's say the blinds are $400/$800 and the ante is $100. With nine players at the table, there will be $2,100 in the pot before the cards are even dealt. If you have a hand that you want to raise with, I suggest making it $2,000 to go.

The so-called *standard raise* would be to $2,400 (three times the big blind), but you can get away with a smaller raise and accomplish the same objective.

With a raise of $2,000, you risk less to win the $2,100 than you risk with the standard raise of $2,400, and you still have a good chance of winning the pot.

2. Protect your chips before protecting the pot

When you're involved in a pot, the first thing to think about is protecting the chips that you already have. Then you can focus on protecting your hand and not losing the pot.

In other words, in a marginal situation where you probably have the best hand but could easily be wrong, err toward the side of caution. Yes, your opponents will outdraw you more often with this approach, but when they do, you'll lose the minimum rather than all the chips in front of you.

For example, suppose you hold pocket aces and the board reads K-K-7-2. If your opponent checks, play cautiously and check as well. If he bets on the river card, you should usually just call and hope that he doesn't have the third king in his hand.

3. Avoid coin flip situations

When you make it all the way to the final table of a tournament, avoid playing large pots in situations where the odds of your winning are about 50-50.

When you have a middle pair versus two higher cards (7-7 versus A-K), you're in the classic coin-flip situation. The best way to stay out of trouble in a marginal scenario like this is to not reraise before the flop. Instead, just call to see the flop.

And don't go crazy with the all-in bets!

If you continually put all your money in before the flop, you're destined to go broke. Sooner or later, your small pair will be in terrible shape against a bigger pair, or you'll find yourself in a coin flip against two overcards. Both are situations that good players try to avoid.

4. Don't bluff too much

If you bluff too much, your table image will be damaged. It will become less and less likely that you'll be able to get away with future bluffs as the tournament progresses.

Small *semibluffs* are okay for the most part, but when you risk a large percentage of your chips, you should rarely be bluffing big.

5. Understand your stack size and never give up

I often see short-stacked players make desperate moves. They think they have no other choice since they're so low on ammunition, but their desperation is often premature.

You needn't be overly concerned with how your chips stack up against the tournament average. It's more important to focus on your stack size in relation to the blinds and antes. For example, if you have $12,000 in chips, and the blinds are $600/$1,200, you only have 10 times the big blind. At that point, you'll need to push it all in when you decide to play a hand.

That doesn't mean you should go all in with a trash hand. You can wait at least one full round before taking your best shot at the pot.

These five tips are the keys to success in deep stack tournaments such as the World Poker Tour and the World Series of Poker. Keep them in mind and you'll outlast much of the competition.

2

Preparing for a Tournament

Poker is clearly not a physical sport, but in order to do well on the major televised poker circuit, top players need to be focused and as physically prepared as possible. The nature of tournament no-limit hold'em is such that a person can play fantastic poker all day long, but make one little mistake and that's it. He's done for.

In fact, to win at the higher levels of competition, players have to be at their best for anywhere from four to five consecutive days. Most tournaments start at noon and don't finish until after midnight. Aside from a one-hour dinner break and ten-minute breathers every couple of hours, there's not much time to rest.

There are a few simple rules that I live by before entering a major event. All of them have served me well. These rules can help you out too in your next tournament, whatever level you play.

1. Get some sleep

You simply cannot play at your best if you're fatigued. You might start out okay, but by hour number eight or nine, you'll start to fade and miss out on a lot that's happening at the table. To be at your best, your brain needs to be alert, spotting tells, focusing on betting patterns, and looking for good bluffing situations. If you're tired, you just won't be able to perform effectively.

2. Don't drink alcohol

You'll hear stories about some hot shot who won a tournament while liquored up the whole way through. Believe me, those victories are few and far between. In a four to five hour span, you might get away with drinking a little alcohol without any serious effect on your results. To win a big tournament, however, you'll have to play consecutive 12-hour days.

Boozing for half the day isn't a good idea for your game or for your health. By the way, I'm not only referring to the actual event. Avoid drinking alcohol the night before an event and during any free time in between your play. Hangovers fog the brain and cost you money.

3. Limit your caffeine

You're going to get tired if you make it deep into a tournament. That's a given. What you do to counteract your fatigue can have a significant impact on your play later in the tournament.

If you're tired near the end of day one, you may think that it's a good idea to get a caffeine jolt from coffee or a Red Bull. While that rush might help you get through the evening, it could have negative consequences if you overindulge in caffeinated beverages, especially on the next day. Coffee dehydrates the body. Drinking too much of it day after day can actually make you groggy. And if you over-caffeinate late in the evening, it will negatively affect your ability to get a good night's sleep.

4. Watch what you eat

Heavy, fatty foods can make you tired. Unfortunately, when you just have ten minutes to grab something on a break, it's likely that you'll only find fast food options such as burgers, pizza or hot dogs.

When you watch me play on television, you'll notice a plastic bag full of goodies that my mother prepares for me. If mommy won't cook for you, then you'd be wise to prepare something light and healthy to get you through until dinner.

At dinner, don't overeat. I can't tell you how many times I've seen players go broke right after the dinner break because they were lethargic from eating a large turkey dinner!

5. Avoid people

This may seem a little strange, but it's amazing how much energy is sucked out of you when you're in large groups listening to poker stories. Hearing slot machines clang or simply engaging in social conversation can also wear you down.

The night before an event, I suggest that you sit alone and quiet your mind. A little light strategy discussion with someone you trust is okay as well, but for the most part, you'll benefit by finding a serene space.

If you are truly serious about doing well in tournaments, you need to prepare properly before the cards are even dealt.

3

Adapt Like a Chameleon

I'm often asked poker strategy questions by amateurs who hope to get concrete answers in return. That's rarely how poker works. There are simply too many variables to consider. The best approach in one situation just might be the absolute worst in another.

In tournament poker, it's not a bad idea to have a game plan right from the start. Unlike football, though, you shouldn't script your first 15 plays of the day as many NFL coaches do. If anything, your game plan must be adaptable to the players that you'll face.

Let's say that you come into a tournament with the following game plan: Sit back early and play conservatively. Then, after a couple of levels, start attacking the blinds. That's not a bad game plan against certain opponents. But what if you find yourself at a table where most of the players simply call before the flop and play very weak after the flop? That type of game requires an immediate change of plans.

When you're up against bad players like these early in a tournament, you shouldn't avoid playing marginal situations. In fact, you should welcome them! If your opponents don't raise before the flop and make big mistakes after the flop, make every attempt to play any two cards that have any value at all. The payoff at a table like this could set you up well for a good run in the tournament.

Now let's analyze the second aspect of the game plan: After a couple of levels, start attacking the blinds. Realistically, that's just not going to work when you're facing weak players. They play too many hands before the flop for this approach to be effective. In other words, they're usually going to call before the flop. So, forget about trying to steal their blinds. Instead, focus on playing well after the flop and taking advantage of your opponents' inexperienced play when it counts.

Let's look at another situation. Three players limp into the pot and you have 8-10 offsuit. This clearly isn't a strong hand; in fact, it's a hand you'd probably never play in a tougher game. But since it's cheap to play, you might as well see a flop and try to get a lucky catch.

The flop comes 9-7-4. The weak field checks the flop all the way around. The turn is a jack giving you the nut straight. If another player has a hand like A-J or K-J, you might just get all of his chips. And all it may cost you was the one bet you called before the flop.

Perhaps you plan to enter the tournament with a completely different game plan, such as: Take control of the table early by raising aggressively before the flop. Keep betting and force your opponents to play defensively.

Once again, that's not a bad plan. But what happens when you find other players at the table using exactly the same game plan to the extreme?

Suppose two or three players are already raising wildly and risking large percentages of their chips on marginal hands. You have a choice to make: Do you go to war with them and risk your tournament life? Or do you wait for these guys to blow each other away and then pick up the pieces on your own terms?

I hope you chose the second option.

You see, there's a pattern here. In football, it's called taking what the defense gives you. Poker works much the same way. When your opponents play too aggressively, take advantage of them by playing with patience. Conversely, when your opponents play weak, become the bull of the table and run right over them. Adapt your game plan as a chameleon changes its colors.

Learning the fundamentals of poker is crucial, but never forget that it's a people game first and a game of math second.

4

Play More Hands in Tournaments

Most no-limit hold'em tournaments have a small blind and a big blind as well as an added ante after the first few rounds. Usually, when the blinds reach $400/$800, each player must contribute a $100 ante. This added expense forces the action a bit, making it difficult for a conservative player to stay afloat while waiting for premium cards.

Waiting around for premium cards is usually not a good strategy. In fact, in tournament play, your goal should be to play more hands than the average player.

In big events, every player knows the difference between great hands, marginal hands, and junk hands. Everyone will play premium hands, most will play marginal hands, and some will even play junk hands if the situation warrants.

Novices should stick to playing premium hands. As you improve and become more comfortable, you can start adding other hands to your repertoire. Bluff attempts to steal the blinds are a great place to start. Just be sure to keep this in mind: There's more to poker than bluffing. The cards you choose to bluff with depend on how well you think you can play each hand after the flop.

Here are some hands you need to consider adding to your game.

Ace-Rag Offsuit

Personally, I hate cards like A♣ 6♦, A♠ 7♥, and A♣ 3♠. They just don't play very well after the flop. If you're lucky enough to flop an ace, your little kicker can cause you big problems.

With a hand like A-7 offsuit, it's unlikely that you'll make a straight or a flush, so you're heavily dependent on catching an ace, or possibly winning unimproved.

However, an ace-high hand plays well *hot and cold*. In other words, with no more betting, it rates to win more often than it loses. In no-limit, though, someone always seems to bet. If a flop comes K-Q-8, you're generally in no-man's-land with ace-rag.

King-Rag and Queen-Rag Suited

Here's another dangerous group of hands to play: K♠ 4♠, K♥ 2♥, Q♦ 6♦, and Q♣ 2♣. The real value in these cards is that they're suited. But that's also the very reason that they're so perilous to play.

Flopping your king or queen is an okay result, but you're really hoping to make a flush. However, even if the flush comes, you could lose all of your chips if an opponent happens to have the ace-high nut flush. Of course, folding a king-high or queen-high flush against a raise is very difficult to do. These hands are certainly playable, but if you go with them, be aware of the potential pitfalls you may encounter.

Small Pairs

Small pairs have loads of value if you're able to see the flop cheaply. They're also easy to play after the flop.

For example, if you call to see the flop with a pair of deuces, you likely will continue only if you hit another 2 on the flop; otherwise, you'll probably fold. If you're lucky enough to catch trips, you're set up to win a big pot, especially if an opponent has a hand like top pair.

Suited Connectors

Hands like 6♥ 7♥ and 3♦ 4♦ are excellent hands to add to your repertoire. Unlike the ace-rag hands, they do play well after the flop because they have both straight and flush potential.

The great thing about these hands is that even if your opponents know you like to play them, you can still win pots with them.

Let's say that you call a raise with 10♠ J♠ and the flop comes 4♣ 5♣ 6♦. Even if your opponent has A-K, he may very well be worried that you've hit that flop. If you bet, you might get him to throw away the better hand.

5

Going All-In Right from the Start

There's a hot topic of debate amongst elite poker professionals: betting it all on a slim margin at the very beginning of a tournament. While some pros have an "all or nothing" mentality about it, others would rather play it more conservatively.

Which one are you?

So here's the situation. You're playing in the $10,000 main event at the World Series of Poker, and you're in the big blind holding the A♦ K♠. Everyone folds, all the way down to the player in the small blind. Now, suppose you could magically see your opponent's cards and know that he has the Q♥ J♥.

Then, in a strange and bizarre move, that player goes all in!

You obviously have him beat, but would you be willing to risk your entire tournament on the very first hand?

Really think about that for a minute.

Let me give you some added insight that might help you make your decision. Your A-K will win the pot 60 percent of the time. This means that if you make this call 10 times, you'll start the main event with a commanding $20,000 in chips on six occasions. The other four times you'll have a day to enjoy the triple-digit summer heat in Vegas.

Having $20,000 in chips early on certainly increases your chances of making the money. No one would be able to knock you out for quite some time. The question you have to ask yourself, though, is whether having those extra chips would justify getting eliminated four times out of ten.

There are other considerations too. How good a player are you? Do you think you're one of the best at the table, or is it likely that you're outclassed?

If you feel like the underdog, you might want to make the call. From a purely mathematical standpoint, it would be foolish to fold your hand. You're a 60 percent favorite on an even money proposition. Vegas casinos survive on much smaller edges than that.

Still, many pros are split on what to do with the hand. Those who believe they are far superior to their opponents claim that they would fold. Their reasoning is twofold: They'll be able to get to $20,000 with much less risk in later play, or they can get all their chips into the pot as a bigger favorite than 60/40.

Where do I stand on the issue? I strongly advise novice and average players to call this hand without hesitation. Yes, there are times when I'd advocate folding, but that would only be at a table with weak players who would let you bully them later.

In televised no-limit tournaments, I'm sure you've seen countless heads-up hands where all the money goes in on percentages close to 50/50. In order to win a tournament, somewhere down the line you're going to have to win a coin flip—a race as it's known in the poker world. You have to get lucky sometimes.

The key is determining when that sometime is the right time.

Why wouldn't you take a guaranteed equitable proposition early on in the tournament? Sixty percent is a substantial favorite in any hold'em hand. The odds in your favor are too good to pass up. This debate will never crown a winner. It really does depend on factors outside of the simple math. The key factor is your ability to objectively gauge your playing skills in comparison to the other players at the table.

So, unless a table is truly ripe for the picking, make the call at 60 percent and look to double up early on. You'll be in a dominant position right from the start.

6

Shootout Tournaments

The World Series of Poker and several other stops on the tournament circuit often hold special "shootout" style events. These are among my favorite games to play.

In a traditional hold'em tournament, if there are 100 entrants, for example, play starts with 10 tables of 10 players each. As soon as 10 players are eliminated, tables are broken up and the remaining competitors fill in seats at the other nine tables. This process continues until there's just one table left, and one player who wins the tournament.

A shootout works differently. A shootout might start with 10 tables of 10 players each, but these tables don't break down as players are eliminated. Instead, each table plays down until one player remains at each of the 10 tables. Those 10 players then move to the final table where each person starts with an equal amount of chips.

In my opinion, shootouts require more skill than traditional tournaments.

To advance in shootouts, players are forced to play well under a variety of circumstances: full-table play, short-handed play, three-handed play, and ultimately, heads-up play. In a traditional tournament, just hanging in there and trying to survive can get you all the way to the final table. Not so in a shootout, because all ten players are in a must-win situation and have to play accordingly.

That's the biggest mistake I see players make in these events. Their mindset is often on surviving, since that's their normal approach to traditional tournament play. In a shootout, however, second place through tenth place pay exactly the same amount—zilch!

The correct approach to winning a shootout (and for that matter, any winner-take-all sit 'n go tournament) is to really go for it. Because the blinds start out small, you can choose to set up a conservative table image that you can look to exploit later. But once the blinds escalate, you need to start dancing.

Sitting back and waiting for others to go broke may work in a typical tournament, but it's a faulty strategy in a shootout. It's all about the top prize, so your game plan should be to play aggressively and take advantage of those who are just trying to survive.

When pros talk about their game, they'll often say something like, "I try to avoid playing coin flip situations with marginal hands." In a shootout, the decision to play marginal hands is irrelevant. Your goal is first place and nothing less. Your sole focus must be on making the correct fundamental plays. If that means you need to gamble all of your chips with pocket fives against A-K in a classic coin flip, then so be it.

Here's a good example of a marginal hand where it makes sense to risk it all in a shootout. You hold J♥ 10♥ and call the raise of a solid player. The flop comes K♥ 7♦ 2♥, giving you a flush draw. Your opponent bets again.

A big raise on your part might be an excellent play. If he's bluffing, or doesn't have a hand such as A-K or better, there's a good chance that he'll fold to your raise. Even if he does call, you'll still have a decent shot at winning a big pot if you complete the flush.

In traditional tournaments, this play is a little too kamikaze for my taste. In shootout formats, it makes a lot of sense and can make you a winner.

7

Two Stack-Building Tricks

The World Series of Poker always draws a mix of entrants: amateurs, professionals, online players, veterans, young guns, women, celebs and sports figures.

Everyone comes into it with his or her own view as to what's the best strategy. Some players bet large sums early in the hand, looking to steal pots before the flop; others only play small pots preflop, trying to win big by taking advantage of their opponents' mistakes after the flop.

There are pros and cons to both strategies.

Being a *dead-money player* means that you're risking large amounts of chips in order to win small pots. It's a very effective strategy that works a high percentage of the time—but when you're wrong it can be very costly.

Let's look at a typical move that a dead-money player might make. With the blinds at $100/$200, and an ante of $25, three players limp into the pot. The small blind calls as well, and now it's up to our dead-money player in the big blind to act. There's already $1,225 in the pot.

The dead-money player often sees this as an opportunity

to steal the pot. Since no one raised before the flop, he may perceive weakness and pounce with a big raise. The key to the play's success is gauging whether the first limper is setting a trap by limping with a big hand. Generally, at least one limper will raise if he has a premium hand. If dead money can get by that first caller, he's probably home free.

The other key consideration is judging the amount of the raise, which is precisely what makes the play risky. Dead money must make a substantial raise to force his opponents out. Making it $600 or $800 to go won't cut it. In order to take the pot right there, he'll probably need to bet about $1,500 in chips.

Betting $1,500 to win $1,225 isn't a bad investment. If he wins the pot two out of three times, he'll make a tidy profit.

Notice, I've never mentioned what hand dead-money holds. Why? Because it simply doesn't matter. He could make this big-blind play with 2-7 offsuit, and many professionals will do just that if they think the moment is right.

While that play can help keep your stack from dwindling, there's another less risky approach to winning. It's known as playing *small ball*. Let's look at an example of how a small ball player plans to build his stack. With the blinds still at $100/$200 and a $25 ante, the small ball player will attack a pot that no one has entered, preferably from late position. His hand doesn't matter all that much, but being suited or connected helps.

Let's say small ball holds the 6♥ 8♥. Rather than call, or make a large raise to steal the blinds, small ball might raise to just $500. He's almost inviting the player in the big blind to call. More often than not, that's exactly what will happen, growing the pot to $1,325.

The flop comes A♠ 9♣ 2♥.

The big blind often will check, and this is where the small ball player must bet despite having nothing at all. A bet of about $800 should do the trick. It will force the big blind to fold unless, of course, he happens to have a pair of aces or better. If that happens, small ball had better fold quickly.

Another advantage to the small ball approach comes when the 6♥ 8♥ actually gets lucky and hits a good flop. If the flop comes 5-7-9, there's no way that any player could figure him for a straight. If his opponent has two pair, trips, or even an overpair, the trap will be set. Small ball will be looking for his big payday.

Both strategies are effective, but the dead-money approach has limited long-term prospects; it's a play that should be used sparingly. It will never win you a huge pot, but could cost you much of your stack.

With the small ball approach, you can accomplish two objectives: You'll continue to build your stack slowly, and occasionally, you'll hit a big flop and double up.

8

Giving Away a Free Card

What you're about to read goes against a strategy often taught in poker literature that recommends a straightforward, all-out aggressive approach when playing in no-limit hold'em tournaments. Undoubtedly, the best approach to no-limit tournaments is to be aggressive, but at the same time, you must avoid major risks in marginal situations. That's what the top pros do.

To help illustrate this concept, there's one specific situation to consider. It relates to flop play. In televised poker tournaments you might hear commentators say something like, "This is a raise or fold situation." Those announcers are often very wrong!

Let's look at an example, and put you in the hand. A player from early position raises to $600 before the flop (blinds are $100/$200). You're in late position holding 9-9 and decide to just call the raise. Many players would tell you to reraise before the flop, but that's not what most pros would do. Instead, professionals want to avoid playing big pots in these marginal situations.

If you reraise, your opponent could go all in. You might

have to fold, only to be bluffed by a hand such as 8-8 or A-K. Or, perhaps you just call and find yourself in a coin flip situation against the A-K. Both are scenarios a top player wants to avoid.

Then the flop comes J♠ 7♦ 4♣, and it's just you and your opponent heads-up. Both of you have about $10,000 in chips and your opponent bets $1,000. You actually have three options here, not just the two that some television pundits suggest. If you're up against a very conservative player who wouldn't bet on the flop unless he has a high pair, you should fold. Or, if you're unsure whether you have the best hand, you can find out with a raise.

The third option, which is usually the best in this situation, is to call the bet on the flop and see what develops on the turn.

Since you have position, you have all the power in the hand. Your opponent has to act first when the remaining cards are dealt, thus giving you valuable information as to what he might have. The obvious problem with just calling the bet is that you're giving your opponent an inexpensive opportunity to outdraw your hand.

This begs a two-part question: How often will calling cause you to lose the pot, and is it worth investing a raise on the flop in a marginal predicament? You can do some simple math to help figure this out. Suppose your opponent holds A-K. He'll catch another ace or king on the turn approximately 14 percent of the time. As an 86 percent favorite, that's a free card I'd willingly give away to avoid playing a big pot on the flop in a problematic situation.

Calling is usually the right play here, but you may still wonder, "How will I know where I'm at in the hand if I don't raise?" Since you have position, you'll usually have a better idea as to whether you're in front after seeing the next card. The problem with raising now is that it costs you chips!

If your opponent bets $1,000 on the flop, you'll have to invest about $3,000 on a raise. That's 30 percent of your chips, which is too much in this dubious situation.

Instead of investing more chips to find out where you're at, it's often better to simply call. You can invest just $1,000 and only give him that slim chance of beating you on the next card. He usually won't get his card, but if he gets lucky and bets the turn, you can safely fold your 9-9, losing only $1,000. If your opponent checks on the turn, you can protect your hand with a bet.

Being aggressive is essential to winning poker tournaments. However, the best players in the world are selectively aggressive and approach marginal situations cautiously. You should do the same.

9

The Stop-and-Go Play

You can use lots of different ploys to win at poker. Among them is a little trick that's very effective in no-limit hold'em tournaments. It's known as the *stop-and-go play*.

You're playing a tournament and are sitting on a short stack in relation to the other players. The blinds are $200/$400 with a $50 ante. You're sitting in the big blind with $3,200 in chips remaining. Everyone folds to the button whose big stack of $82,000 dominates. He raises the pot to $1,200. The small blind folds.

You have A-Q in the hole and it's up to you to act. You think it's the best hand. The dilemma you face is whether to go all-in and raise with your last $2,000, or just call the bet and see what the flop brings. I'll bet that most players would probably move all-in before the flop. After you read this chapter, though, you'll understand why it's often much better to call and see the flop.

Assume that the button is on a steal-raise. Since he has so many chips, he'll likely call your $2,000 reraise with virtually any two cards. If he calls the raise with a hand such as K-10, he'll get to look at all five community cards, and he'll also knock you out of the tournament about 38 percent of the time.

Moving all in preflop is the correct play in some situations, but not in this case. Your opponent would only have to call $2,000 to win about $5,000. Not many hands are that much of an underdog before the flop. In fact, calling with a hand as lousy as 2-3 offsuit wouldn't be such a bad idea—even it will beat A-K over 34 percent of the time.

Okay, now that we've established that your opponent will usually call your all-in raise, why wouldn't you want that to happen if you think A-Q is the best hand?

Remember that tournament poker is all about survival. Sometimes you must sacrifice value in order to survive. In this case, if you wait until after the flop, you can actually increase your chances of winning the pot.

Here's where you can use the stop-and-go play. Instead of going all in before the flop, just call the $1,200 raise from the player on the button. You can use your remaining $2,000 to (hopefully) force your opponent out later in the hand. Keep in mind, though, that when you make the call before the flop, you must be committed to moving the rest of your chips all in regardless of what comes on the flop. The only time you might want to stray from this plan is when you flop a very strong hand.

When that doesn't happen—the flop comes something such as 9-6-4, 8-3-3, or even K-7-2—bet your last $2,000 immediately, hoping that your opponent will fold. You may even be able to bluff him out. For example, if the flop comes J-10-9 and your opponent has a pair of fours, he'll probably just give up right there.

Now, if your opponent holds the K-10, the flop comes 9-6-4, and he calls your $2,000 bet, he'll only win the pot approximately 25 percent of the time. Calling would be a mistake for him and you would benefit.

Stop-and-go play not only increases your chances of survival, it can force your opponent into making mistakes after the flop. If you move all in before the flop, your opponent would be absolutely correct to call with his K-10, but he'd be making an error if he called after the flop.

The fundamental theorem of poker, coined by author David Sklansky, dictates that anytime your opponent plays a hand differently than he would have if he could see your cards, you gain.

Based on that theory, stop-and-go play offers more opportunities for your opponent to make a mistake. Because you've already made your decision before the flop, putting in your last chips after that juncture doesn't require much thought. Your opponent, however, still has to make a difficult decision that he wouldn't have faced earlier.

10

Getting to the River is Half the Battle

Playing in a no-limit hold'em tournament is much different from playing in a cash game. In cash games, your goal is simply to play each hand optimally, thinking only about getting maximum value for each hand while minimizing your losses. But in tournaments, great players avoid thin edges and play marginal hands extra carefully. By doing this, they often sacrifice a little bit of value in order to protect themselves from losing a big pot.

Have you ever been in a hand where your opponent bets the turn and you're almost certain you have the best hand? Here's the predicament: If you raise and are wrong, it can cost you all your chips. This is the kind of scenario that separates skilled players from those who don't fully understand the nuances of tournament play.

Let's look at an example. You raise with the A♠ J♦ and one player calls. The flop comes J♠ 6♦ 2♥ and your opponent checks. You bet out and he calls. The turn card is the 7♦. Your opponent decides to bet.

A play like this usually means one of the following things:

- He flopped trips and was slowplaying on the flop
- He made two pair with a hand such as 6-7
- He too has flopped a pair of jacks, but with a small kicker; he's trying to protect his hand
- He has a pocket pair such as 10-10 and is trying to find out where you're at
- He's just bluffing

As you can see, you're in terrible shape against some of these hands, while others give your opponent very few outs to beat you. Regardless of which hand you think he has, this is a situation where your goal should be to get to the river as cheaply as possible. And that's why raising would definitely be the wrong play.

Against trips, you'd be drawing nearly dead. Against two pair, you'd need to catch an ace, jack, or a deuce to win. Against another jack with a weaker kicker, you're ahead now, but he has outs to beat you. Against pocket tens, only two cards in the deck can beat you; if you raise here, he'll certainly fold. Against the bluff, you'll let him off the hook with a raise. He'll fold instead of possibly continuing his bluff on the river.

Anytime you play a hand post-flop in a no-limit hold'em tournament, the pot is usually quite large. Do everything you can to make sure that you don't get bluffed out or make the pot any bigger than necessary.

Consider this scenario. You raise with K-K and get one caller. The flop comes A♠ 9♣ 2♦. Ideally, you'd want to take this hand to the river with no betting at all. Yes, pocket kings are very strong, but that ace is a scary card; you don't want to see an opponent bet at any point. If the hand is checked all the way to the river, consider it a victory in a very risky situation.

It's true that aggressive play is important in tournaments. However, it's equally important to know when not to be aggressive. Understand that concept and you'll recognize when it's better to proceed with caution.

Strong players are aggressive before the flop, stealing lots of blinds and antes. On top of that, they'll usually have the goods when they get to post-flop play. You can become that kind of player by controlling the action to the river. Make it that far and your battle is almost won.

11

Defense Wins Championships

You've probably heard that defense wins in the sports world, especially football. But this is probably the first time that you've heard it associated with playing the World Poker Tour. As in team sports, poker offense is a lot more flashy and exciting to watch, but it's defense that gets you the title and millions in prize money. When you think of offense in poker you think of raising and reraising, or maybe making some big bluffs. That might make for good television, but it's not going to help you get to the final table.

There's a misconception about how top professionals get to the money more often than others. They aren't doing it with wild bluffs that risk large percentages of their stacks. The real key to their long-term success and consistency is playing solid defense.

In poker, playing defensively is often considered weak. If you consider guys like Phil Ivey, Gus Hansen and me to be weak players at the poker table, then you just don't understand the reasoning behind cautious play in large pots.

Let's look at an example that puts you in the hand. A player raises your big blind and you defend it with A-J. The flop comes A♣ 9♠ 4♦. You check to your opponent. If he bets half of the pot, what would you do?

The "strong" or offensive play is to check-raise the flop, while the "weak" or defensive play is to check and call. In this case, the best play is usually to take the cautious approach. You have a strong hand with aces and a decent kicker, but it's far from the nuts. If your opponent has A-K, A-Q, two pair, or a set, you're in deep trouble. By playing cautiously, you hope to accomplish two things: rope your opponent in by letting him try to bluff you out of the hand, and more importantly, minimize your loss on the hand when you are beaten.

Of course, the one potential negative you allow by not raising on the flop is letting your opponent catch a card to beat you.

However, with a board like A-9-4, what card does he need if he doesn't have you beaten already? If he has A-10, only one of three 10s remain in the deck to beat you. Or if he has K-K, he only has two remaining outs to win.

Here's another example. You hold the Q♥ 10♥ and the flop comes 9♠ 4♥ 8♥. The turn card is the 4♦, and the river comes the 5♥, giving you a queen-high flush. All along, your opponent has been betting at you. On the river, he once again leads out and bets the size of the pot. You just hit your flush, so what should you do?

You only have two good options: call or fold. Raising would be an offensive play, but it would often be a bad idea. If your opponent has bet all the way and still bets the river card, you have to consider that you may be beaten by a higher flush or even a full house. If you decide to raise, chances are that your opponent will only call when he has you beat, thus giving no positive value to your raise. You lose more when you're beaten, and win no more when you have the best hand.

I see many young players overplaying their hands before

and after the flop. They needlessly go broke in situations where a more experienced player would have been thinking defense.

Your main objective in a tournament is to survive longer than everyone else and eventually win all the chips. You can't win the tournament in the early stages, but you can get yourself knocked out foolishly if you aren't thinking defense first.

12

Three Keys to Final Table Strategy

Poker books go into great detail discussing the various strategies necessary to get to the final table of a tournament. Not as much has been written about final table playing strategy. Here are some tips to help you make it from the final table to the winner's circle.

1. Take what the table gives

This is a simple concept but one that can't be overlooked. This philosophy applies not only to poker, but also to football and basketball. Sometimes, late in an NFL game, the team protecting its lead will often go into a prevent defense, trying to defend against the long pass. Trying to throw a bomb against that type of coverage isn't a very good idea. Instead, the opponent takes what the defense gives, and throws shorter passes while continuing to move the chains.

In the NBA, Kobe Bryant has the ability to blow right past players who guard him too closely. But if someone lays off him, he'll just pull up and shoot a jump shot.

Pretend for a second that you're the Lakers star, and the

defense is playing tight and guarding the rim. They're giving you an open look at a 15-foot jumper! Would you try to drive the lane or take the easy shot? I hope you said the easy shot.

At the final table of a poker tournament, you also must base your choices on how your opponents are playing—in other words, what they're giving you. If the table is playing passively, and everyone is waiting for others to get knocked out, that's your cue to drive the lane and play aggressively.

Conversely, if there are overly aggressive, wild players at your table, then the best course of action is to sit back and wait for them to pick each other off.

You cannot win a tournament in one hand when there are still nine players at the table. So, your goal in the early stages of final table play is to set yourself up for the short-handed battle to come.

2. Adjust

One of the most difficult challenges novices face at a final table is making the necessary adjustments for short-handed play. During most tournaments, play is nine-handed all the way down to the final table. As you get down to six, five, or four players, though, the correct playing strategy will change dramatically.

It's true that a player may succeed by waiting for premium starting cards on his way to the final table. However, if he continues playing that way short-handed, the blinds and antes will eat away at his stack.

Hands such as A-7 offsuit, cards you wouldn't play in a nine-handed game, become raisers when play becomes short-handed. To stay afloat, you need to win one set of blinds per round. If you're playing four-handed, that means you need to pick up a pot in one out of every four hands. If you fold A-7, you may not get a better chance for a while.

3. Play the players and your stack

The cards become less important at the final table than they were in the early stages of a tournament. At the final table, shift your focus to determine who you can steal pots from and who you can trap. You've got to play the players.

Unfortunately, it's difficult to play the players when you don't have many chips. If you're on the short stack, you'll be forced to sit back and wait for a good opportunity to either double up or steal the blinds.

It's a much rosier picture if you're one of the bigger stacks at the final table. Then you have virtual free reign to attack and pressure your opponents. There's no need to be reckless. The other players will be forced to respect your stack size since any hand they play could be their last.

Now let's review. Let the game come to you in the early stages. Make the necessary adjustments once play becomes short-handed. Finally, always be aware of your stack size in relation to the others.

If you focus on those three key elements, you'll often find yourself playing heads-up for the title.

13

When to Be Aggressive in Tournament Play

Poker books and television commentators constantly preach to players about the importance of aggressive play. However, playing cautiously is often equally important. It's critical that you're able to figure out both styles of play. Let's look at various scenarios and decide where aggressive play is better than cautious play.

Playing a Big Stack Against Another Big Stack

If you find yourself with a big stack of chips playing against another chip leader, common sense should tell you to proceed cautiously. In this situation, protecting your stack is more important than playing aggressively.

Playing an opponent who can put a huge dent in your stack is fraught with danger—your big stack can suddenly become the short stack.

Playing from the Dealer Button

The button is a position of power. It's also a good time to be aggressive. As a rule, you can get away with playing more hands in the later positions than you can in earlier positions. You have more information at your disposal to make good decisions because your opponents always have to act first.

In fact, when you're in position, the quality of your hand is often meaningless since you'll be playing the players rather than the cards. A good way to practice is to play the button without even looking at your cards. Instead, focus on your opponents and try to figure out if they're strong or weak. If you sense weakness, make a bet and they'll likely fold.

Of course, if you think someone has a strong hand, forget the practice. That would be a good time to take a look at your cards.

Playing Top Pair After the Flop

This is the one situation where many players go wrong. They play too aggressively when they flop top pair or have an overpair to the board. Top pair is often a strong hand in small pots, but if the pot gets large and opponents are playing aggressively, slow down! You should certainly bet on the flop, but be cautious if you get any resistance.

Playing Monster Draws After the Flop

Monster draws include a pair with a flush draw, a straight and a flush draw, a straight-flush draw, and flush or straight draws with overcards. These are usually powerful hands. Even when you're forced into playing a big pot, your odds of winning are still very good. For that reason, you can afford to be aggressive with monster draws after the flop.

Aggressive play gives you two ways to win the pot: Your bet gets everyone to fold, or you end up improving your hand and winning the pot anyway.

Near-the-Money Payouts

In a tournament with 300 players, usually the top 27 will

finish in the prize money. Because of this, when there are about 30 competitors left, play becomes extremely cautious as many people are hoping to hang on for a money finish.

It is at this precise moment that you should seize the opportunity to steal as many chips as possible.

Play aggressively against those players trying to squeak into the money. Yes, this does increase the possibility that you'll knock yourself out of the money, but in the long run it pays off. You give yourself a chance to hit one of the top three spots, and that's where the lion's share of the money is in tournament poker.

PART II:
PLAYING YOUR PLAYERS, YOUR POSITION AND (OH, YES) YOUR CARDS

Hold'em is a people game played with cards. Does that sound backwards to you? Not at all. Once you get to know your opponents, you can decide how to best play against them, depending on your seat position at the table. Here are some of my top tips on how to identify and win against different types of players, and how to keep them guessing about what you're going to do next.

14

Reading Your Opponents

The questions that I'm probably asked the most are, "How do you read players, and how do you figure out what they have?" The world's greatest poker players can read their opponents like a book. They happen to be great human lie detectors.

There is no secret, earth-shattering formula to put opponents on a hand, but there are some things you should look for when sizing them up. It isn't magic, though, as there are several key tip-offs that you can look for when trying to read opponents.

1. What are they wearing?

Clothing choice and personal appearance can often tell you something about a player's approach to poker. An opponent who is clean-shaven, has neat hair, and wears traditional clothing reveals plenty about his personality. This player leans toward the conservative, and chances are good that his poker game will mimic his outward appearance.

Conversely, if your opponent wears a stained shirt, has uncombed hair and a five-o'clock shadow, and is generally not "put together," his poker-playing style is likely to be wild, loose and unpredictable.

However, like anything else, there are exceptions to the rules, so any form of player stereotyping should be done cautiously.

2. What do they do for a living?

Obviously, if your opponent is a professional poker player, you can safely make some assumptions as to how he plays the game. For one, he'll take it seriously—he's much less likely to play wildly. He'll usually play poker by the book.

A professional's style makes fundamental sense; for this reason alone, it's often easier to narrow down a pro's possible holding than that of a novice. Caveat: That doesn't mean that it's easier to play against a pro. Trust me, it isn't.

I'll often ask my opponents what they do for a living. It gives me information that can reveal personality traits. For example, if I discover that a woman at my table is a Sunday school teacher, I'd be more apt to think that she's less likely to bluff. Why? She may feel personally conflicted about bluffing, who knows?

If I'm up against a lawyer, you can bet I'll be on my toes. Years of playing against them have taught me that they're more likely to bluff. Bluffing is like telling a story; all of the facts must add up so that an opponent believes you have a strong hand. That kind of thought process is second nature to most lawyers.

Certain physical tells can also tell you plenty. Here are five tells to get you started.

3. When a player glances at his chips, it's usually a sign of strength

You're playing Texas hold'em and when the flop is dealt, you notice that your opponent quickly looks down at his chips. This tell is very common, especially among novice players. Why?

It's a purely subconscious reaction. When the flop comes giving you a great hand, your brain sends out a signal to check the size of your stack to see how much you can bet. Players don't even realize that they do it, but they do. Be observant and you'll catch it every time.

As soon as the flop hits, the eyes of a player who makes his hand will quickly dart towards his chips and then back up again.

4. Strong means weak and weak means strong

This is another common tell that you can spot in several forms. It can be the way a player throws his chips into the pot or the tone of his voice that gives away his hand.

When a player sounds dejected, saying something like, "Well, I guess it's now or never; I might as well bet all of my chips," that's usually a sign that he holds a powerful hand. He's trying to sound weak so he doesn't scare you off. Trust me, he'll show you a full house if you call him!

Another way to spot this tell is to watch how an opponent puts his chips into the pot. Did he forcefully throw his chips toward you, or did he gently place a stack in the pot?

When a player throws his chips in an aggressive manner, he's trying to scare you. He probably has a weak hand. On the flipside, when he gently places his bet in the pot, he likely has something strong and he's inviting you into the pot, hoping that you'll call.

5. A player who makes no sense at all is usually nervous and a bluffer

While playing, I'll often ask competitors questions to gauge their responses. If someone responds incoherently, it's generally a sign of nervousness that comes from bluffing. Conversely, if an opponent is very calm when answering, he probably has a strong hand. Most likely, you're beat.

6. A player suddenly changes his behavior

When a normally talkative player suddenly has nothing to say, you can be sure he's bluffing. In fact, anytime a player does something that appears to be out of the ordinary for him, it's generally a clue that he's bluffing.

7. Body language reveals a lot

When a player bluffs, he'll often curl up into a ball, literally or figuratively, hoping to avoid bringing any attention to himself. For instance, if you play with a guy who smokes, watch the way he pulls a drag from his cigarette after he makes a bet. If he takes a deep drag and blows out a big cloud of smoke, it's often a sign of strength. He's comfortable.

On the other hand, if that same guy pushes a big bet into the pot, takes a drag, and then barely blows out any smoke, he's bluffing. He doesn't want to bring any attention to himself so he tenses up. Often, he'll look very stiff and unnatural.

These tips should help you pick off a timely bluff or two, but it's important to note that each individual tip, while taken alone, cannot be counted on for complete accuracy.

Reading physical tells will certainly make you a better player, but the only way to become a great player is to master the fundamentals of the game. Mastering the basics will give you an edge in figuring out your best move against your opponents. Noting the hands that your opponents play is one of the important fundamentals of any poker game.

8. What kinds of hands do they play?

Whatever your opponents' profession or physical tells, you still need to look for clues that can help steer your decision in a big pot. You do that by paying close attention to the hands your opponents play. Ultimately, it's much more important than how they dress or the type of work they do.

Let's say that you know that an opponent likes to limp in

from early position with small pairs, but when he has an A-K or A-Q, he'll raise. Also, you know he won't play hands such as 5-6 or A-6 suited in that position.

Suppose you have A-K and the flop comes A♣ 6♦ 4♠. If that opponent check-raises you on the flop, you might be able to save a lot of money. Sure, you have a great hand with top pair and top kicker, but because you know your opponent's tendencies, you'll be able to fold, realizing that his most likely hand is 4-4 or 6-6.

People will be amazed when you say to him, "Pocket fours or pocket sixes, right?" Because you have a solid read on the cards he likes to play, it was hardly magic at all. It was actually rather obvious.

In addition to learning the hands people play before the flop, it's also important to study how your opponents play certain hands in different situations. The definitive skill to reading opponents is being able to figure out what type of plays they're capable of making. Learn that and you'll also know what plays they would never make.

15

The Silent Dialog in Limit Hold'em

Limit hold'em is a beautiful game to play. Maybe it's not as dramatic as no-limit with those exciting all-in bets, but the betting in limit hold'em has a flow to it that's like a language of its own. This dialog is non-verbal but it speaks volumes. Let me illustrate this point by reviewing the betting in a typical hand.

Playing a $10/$20 limit cash game, Charlie raises the pot before the flop to $20 from middle position. That bet says, *I have the best hand boys, and I'm going to attack those blinds.* Then Joe reraises the bet to $30 from the dealer position: *Sorry Charlie, I think I'm the one with the best hand.* All the other players fold.

The flop comes K♠ 8♦ 4♣. Charlie is first to act and checks. He's saying, O*kay, tough guy, since you reraised me before the flop, go ahead and bet.*

Joe isn't ready to slow down just yet. He bets: *Charlie, I'm not scared of that king. Who knows, I might even have one myself.*

Having made the obligatory check to the raiser, Charlie now fires back a raise at Joe. *Not so fast Joe, I liked that flop and I'm ready to dance. You game? Let's make it $20.*

Joe stares at Charlie and reaches for more chips. *What,*

did you think I was kidding, Charlie? When I said I had the best hand, I meant it. Joe verbally announces "Reraise!" as he fires his chips into the pot.

The action gets back to Charlie, who decides to just call. *All right Joe, I'll stop raising … for now. But I'm not letting you have this pot just yet. Let's see another card.*

The turn card is the 2♣.

This part of the unspoken poker conversation should usually go the same way for Charlie. Since he didn't reraise on the flop, he should check the turn. Otherwise, the conversation just doesn't flow; if Charlie were to bet, it just wouldn't make much sense.

But he does anyway. *Um…er, I know you reraised me on the flop but I'm still going to bet.*

Joe glances back at Charlie with a puzzled look on his face. *Now you're betting? You didn't reraise me to $40 on the flop, and all of a sudden I'm supposed to believe that a deuce helped? If it did help you, why wouldn't you check-raise me? You know I'm going to bet for sure.*

Here's the way the hand is supposed to play out. Either Charlie should make it $40 and bet the turn, or he should just call the $30 and check. Any other play doesn't go with the flow of the conversation.

This is what Charlie should have said to himself: *Okay Joe, you go ahead and bet and we'll see what I decide to do. I might be trapping you, or I might be a little scared. You'll never know which it is.*

Joe then bets the turn. *I'm not scared of a little old deuce, and I've got a monster hand. Let's make it $20 to go.*

Charlie then springs back into action. *Gotcha! I'm the man with the best hand and here's $40 to prove it.*

Joe makes the reluctant call. *Wow, Charlie, it looks like maybe you do have the best hand, but I'm going to pay the price to see it.*

The river card is another deuce, and Charlie makes his last bet at the pot. *I wasn't kidding and I'm not stopping now.*

Once again, Joe calls. *I guess you might have me beat, Charlie, but the pot is too big now, I have to call you.*

Charlie then turns over pocket eights for a full house. Joe sends his hand to the muck face up: big slick, A-K.

The combination of betting and non-verbal dialog made sense throughout the hand. When professionals play limit hold'em, all the bets seem to have a rhythm that makes sense. Every action has a meaning, and it's usually predicated on the play from the previous street.

Playing wildly may help you win some no-limit hands, but limit poker is more of a science than an art. Both are beautiful games, but a different approach is required for each one.

16

Exploiting Weak-Tight Players

Whether you're playing a big no-limit hold'em tournament or just enjoying a home game with friends, invariably you'll come across a player that falls under the category of *weak-tight*. Let's define the terms.

Weak describes how an opponent plays his hands, more so after the flop than before it. A weak player misses too many bets and gives away too many free cards. He's essentially afraid of his own shadow.

Tight describes the player's hand selection before the flop. A tight player is extremely conservative before the flop, only playing premium hands in good position

Being a weak-tight player is the absolute worst approach you can have if you plan to win a tournament with hundreds of entrants. To win large field tourneys, it's imperative that you're active in lots of pots. That helps build a monster stack.

Simply waiting for premium hands and then playing them weakly after the flop, is a recipe for disaster. You won't get enough quality hands to survive the escalating blinds. Also, if you play your hands poorly after the flop you won't win enough chips to make a run in the tournament.

Mind you, if your goal is to simply last for a long time in a tournament with little chance to win but a decent shot to squeak into the money, a weak-tight approach will help you accomplish that goal.

Consider yourself lucky when you're at a tournament table against weak-tight players. Play your cards properly—or more importantly, their cards properly—and you'll be able to steal your way to a big stack with very little risk.

You should aggressively target weak-tight players, especially in tournaments when you need to pick up small pots to help build your stack. Focus on these four tips to best exploit them.

1. Relentlessly attack them preflop and on the flop

This type of opponent is always waiting for quality hands. Since we know that he'll seldom get one, put the pedal to the metal and raise his blinds like a bank robber in the middle of the day.

2. Don't pay off a weak-tight player

The last thing you ever want to do is lose a big pot to one of these guys. They always have a strong hand. Even if you make a king-high flush, be wary. If he raises you, he likely has an ace-high flush.

3. Play small pots

The best way to exploit the weak-tight player is to control the pot size. Unless you have the absolute nuts, attack small pots while avoiding the big ones. Weak-tight players willingly allow you to chop away at small pots. They're hoping that you'll eventually lose a monster pot to them when they show you the stones.

4. Shut down on the turn if you get action

If you aren't able to win the pot on the flop, you probably need to abort mission. If your opponent calls all the way to the turn, there's no doubt that he has a strong hand. It's going to be a rare occurrence when he starts with a premium hand and then catches a good flop. But when he does, don't get stubborn and try to take the pot away from him. You'll have ample opportunities to chop away at smaller pots later on with minimal risk.

To beat a weak-tight player you need to understand his game plan. He won't bluff, he'll only play premium hands, and he'll avoid marginal situations. Understanding that mental approach makes it very easy to beat him, regardless of which cards you're actually dealt.

You're not playing your cards, you're playing his!

17

Five Keys to Playing Against Tough Opponents

Ideally you want to play in games where you're clearly the best player at the table. In no-limit hold'em tournaments, however, you don't have the luxury of choosing which table you'll be playing at. Unless you truly believe that you're the absolute best poker player on the planet—you're not!—here are some adjustments to make when playing against superior opponents.

Make Larger Preflop Raises

As a rule, I'm a big advocate of making small raises before the flop rather than oversized ones. However, when you're facing tough players, you should be seeing fewer flops and be willing to risk a few more chips in order to steal the blinds. This is especially true when facing a tough player in the big blind.

Tough players are notorious blind defenders who play well after the flop. So, avoid marginal situations against them by making slightly larger preflop raises in an attempt to get them to fold.

For example, if your standard raise is about three times the big blind, increase it to four times when a strong player is in the big blind. With a hand such as 8-8 or A-Q, you'd be better off picking up the blinds with no resistance rather than playing a flop against this tough opponent.

Avoid Marginal Situations

If a tough player raises from early position, don't call him with marginal hands like K-J or Q-10. Those hands aren't very good in any situation, but they're especially vulnerable against a great player who isn't going to make many mistakes after the flop.

Target Weaker Players

Look to play more hands against the less-skilled players at your table. If that means stretching your starting hand requirements against them, then that's what you need to do. In fact, you'd be much better off playing a hand such as 5♣ 3♣ against a weaker player than you would be by playing a hand such as A-10 against a top player.

Against the weak player, you'll be able to outplay him after the flop by bluffing or by getting him to pay you off when you have him crushed. That's not the case when you're up against a player who might be better than you. Here, you run the all-too-likely risk of being outplayed yourself.

Don't Get Too Cute

One of the biggest mistakes players make when they're outclassed is that they add too much trickery to their game in the hope of outplaying a better opponent.

Give it up.

Your focus should be on playing fundamentally sound poker. If you do, it will be difficult for a better player to exploit you. When you get too creative in an attempt to fool him, he'll usually see right through the play and turn the tables on you.

Play Cautiously

Don't play big tournament pots against the best player at your table unless you have a monster hand. Sure, you eventually must beat all of the players in order to get the first place trophy, but it's a better policy to worry about them later rather than sooner. You can even hope that the best player takes a bad beat from one of the weaker opponents. Those are chips you can more easily pick up.

Even if you have a very strong hand on the river—one that you're fairly sure beats your opponent—take the safe route and call him rather than raise.

There is less value in raising a great player on the river because it could cost you all of your chips if he does have you beat. Besides, when you do have the better hand, a great player won't call your raise anyway.

Here's the bottom line: Don't play scared poker, but when you spot a strong opponent, choose your battles wisely.

18

Playing Against a Poker Maniac

A question I'm often asked is, "How do I deal with a maniac who is playing every hand?" Before I can answer that question properly, I need more information on the type of maniac you are dealing with. Not all maniacs are created equal. Each has his own personal tendencies. Some may play poorly while others may have excellent instincts and card reading skills.

The Habitual Bluffer

The easiest maniac to defend against is the habitual bluffer who is a lifelong losing player. In fact, it's simple to play against such a player. Here are a few basic tips to consider.

1. Isolate him

When he raises, reraise with any hand that is good enough to see the flop with. He will be raising with hands such as K-4, so when you pick up a hand such as A-J, go ahead and try to play heads-up against him.

2. Don't give him any credit

A leopard can't change his spots, and a habitual bluffer can't resist the temptation to bluff, even in the most obvious situations. When you have a hand that could win in a showdown, you have to at least call your opponent down to the river card.

3. Let him bluff off his money

When you are dealt a strong hand against this type of player, set a trap for him by slowplaying your hand. He'll almost always go for the bait when you check to him because he thinks that he can steal the pot from you. So, set the hook and reel in his chips.

The Crazy-Like-a-Fox Opponent

The more difficult opponent to play against often isn't a maniac at all. He's just fooled you into believing that he is a crazy wild man. He's crazy, alright, crazy like a fox. In reality, he is an excellent reader of cards and people. These poker skills allow him to play more hands than a typical player.

Battling this type of player can be very tricky. Consider these tips when seated at a table with a sly fox who seems to be dominating the game.

1. Don't be fooled by his starting hand selection

Often, he'll try to disguise his level of skill by revealing a trash hand in a situation most would never dream of playing. For example, he may reraise from the big blind with a hand such as 7-2.

Some players may incorrectly jump the gun and conclude that this player is a fool who has no idea what he is doing. Be careful: Never judge a player's skill level based on his play before the flop.

2. Get position on him

Consistently being out of position against this type of player can be a nightmare and is a recipe for disaster. Because he will be active in a lot of pots, it's important that you try to sit to his left, so that he'll have to act before you on every street. This will neutralize his advantage over you, if he has an advantage at all.

3. Isolate him

Don't be quite as adventurous with the cards you choose to play. Make sure that you have a hand that plays well after the flop and will be competitive in a heads-up showdown.

4. Beware of falling for the "advertising" trap

Early in the game, this player will often reveal a monster bluff that he was able to win. It's very important to understand that he's doing this for a specific reason; it's not that he's just showing off. More often than not, he will show an early bluff to train his opponents to consistently pay him off when he gets strong hands later in the game. Keep in mind that he has virtually no plan to attempt another "reckless" bluff for the rest of the night.

Contrary to the strategy to be employed against the loose maniac, give the smart player more credit when he is investing a lot of bets in a pot. After he's shown a bluff or two, the chances significantly decrease that he'll bluff in that same situation again.

19

Kamikaze All-In Plays

When watching poker tournaments on television, you'll invariably see a hand where a player makes a reraise for all of his chips with an absolutely terrible hand. The commentators will marvel about how great a play it was, but I promise you this: Kamikaze all-in plays with garbage hands will get you eliminated from tournaments far more often than they will work in your favor.

I wouldn't, however, eliminate the reraise-with-garbage tactic from your repertoire. Instead, think about making this play only when the worst-case outcome would not result in a catastrophic hit to your stack.

Let's say the blinds are $400/$800 with a $100 ante and you're sitting on $100,000 in chips. A player from late position raises to $2,400. You suspect that he's attempting to steal the blinds.

In this example, consider trying to re-steal the pot, even if you have a hand as bad as 2-7. You'll have to make a large reraise, though, as you definitely don't want your opponent to call and see the flop. Try raising it $10,000 more. With $12,400 in the pot, you'd be risking just 12.4 percent of your stack. If your play works, you'd increase your stack by 4.5 percent and that's not bad.

Now, if you only have $12,400 chips instead of $100,000, this play would be far too risky for a couple of reasons. First, a player who has not yet acted just might call your bet with a playable hand. Or, the original raiser might have a strong hand himself. It's also possible that even if the original raiser's hand isn't particularly strong, he'll still call since it won't cost him much to try to eliminate an opponent.

Position is of utmost importance when using this tactic. It works best from the button or the blinds since you significantly reduce the chance of having another player call your bet.

How about when you're playing on a short stack? That's when it's most imperative that you protect those precious chips. Make sure that when you attempt a last ditch effort to double up, you have a hand that will be competitive in an all-in situation.

Amateur players tend to give up way too early when their chip stacks dwindle, and that's a big mistake. It's amazing how quickly things can turn around if you're patient and wait for decent opportunities to play your remaining chips.

It's actually fairly simple to play a short stack in a tournament because there are so few poker weapons at your disposal. Yes, some players consider the kamikaze all-in bluff a weapon—but not me. When your tournament life is on the line, it's a play that you should avoid at all costs. It's much wiser to pay close attention to the action and look for a good situation to make your move.

Remember, too, that it's difficult to steal blinds as a short stack. So, when your chip stack dips to less than 10 times the big blind and you decide to play a hand, be aggressive and go all-in rather than make a standard raise of three times the big blind. Ideally, you'll end up in a situation where you won't mind if your bet is called because your hand rates to be the best. If everyone folds, that's not a horrible result either. Eventually, though, you'll need to win a race for all of your chips in order to get back into contention.

Patience is often rewarded when you're a short stack. Let the quitters make the kamikaze all-in plays while you sit tight looking for that solid opportunity to double up.

20

Three Ways to Add Deception to Your Game

The key to becoming a winning poker player is to learn the fundamentals that will make your game consistently strong. Once you do that, and become a winning player in smaller games, you'll need to add some deception to your game in order to compete at higher levels.

A straightforward ABC strategy works against average players. However, against more perceptive opponents, you'll need deception to keep them from easily getting a read on your play. Let's look at a few methods.

1. Slowplay aces

You can slowplay aces several ways, making this an effective ploy from time to time. One method is to limp in by just calling the opening bet rather than raising. Limping in usually signifies a weaker hand like small suited connectors or small pairs.

By limping in with aces you might entice another player to raise before the flop. He may figure you for a weaker hand. At that point, you can reraise before the flop, or you can continue slowplaying the hand until the flop hits.

But what if there's been a preflop raise?

In that case, another tricky way to play pocket aces is by only calling an opponent's preflop raise. Since opponents are likely to believe that you'd reraise with aces, smooth calling helps to disguise the power of your hand. Even if they catch on to the fact that you occasionally make these plays, it will help to keep them off your back; they won't know if you have 8♠ 9♠ or A-A, since you're willing to play both hands the same way.

2. Raise with suited connectors from early position

When a good player raises from early position, it's correct to assume that he has a strong hand. Knowing that, you should fold hands such as K-J or K-Q after an early position raise.

However, when you're that early position player, you can't play it too ABC. You won't get maximum value for your better hands because opponents will know that you only play strong cards from early position. Raising with hands such as 6♠ 7♠ or 8♥ 9♥ will be completely unexpected.

You might even get lucky and hit a straight or trips on the flop and end up winning a huge pot.

The good news is that even if you get caught raising with one of these early position hands, it should help you get more action later on when you raise with strong cards. Your opponents will always be wondering if it's A-K that you have, or 4♥ 5♥.

3. Show an occasional bluff

Be careful about giving away free information about your hands, but if your opponents catch on to the fact that you're playing tight, it might be a good idea to show them a well-timed bluff.

Revealing your bluff will keep them guessing and should allow you to go back to playing your normal, straightforward style. In fact, you don't have to stop there. Anytime you make an uncharacteristic play—a move that you don't plan on making for the rest of the session—show your hand. It's something that you can exploit later.

Always keep this in mind: Mixing up your play is an inexact science. It's hard to know when it's the right time to throw in deceptive plays, but as you gain more experience, it'll be easier to spot the best situations to try them.

Just be very careful not to overdo it. Deceptive play is most effective when seldom employed.

21

Playing from the Small Blind

Playing correctly from the small blind is the poker topic that's been least covered in instructional poker media. Most books discuss position, starting hand requirements and pot odds, but I've yet to see much solid information on how to play from the small blind. The correct strategy from this position might surprise you. You see, there are two contrasting facts to ponder: You already have half of the bet in, but you have the worst position after the flop. The first situation is favorable; the second is not.

When facing a preflop raise, especially from a player in one of the early positions, play conservatively from the small blind. Forget that you're getting a bit of a discount. However, if you're dealt a premium hand in this situation, you must reraise. It's the only play that somewhat neutralizes your positional disadvantage.

In limit hold'em, raising helps give you control of the hand. In no-limit, a large preflop raise might just win you the pot right there.

Some players smooth call early position raises from the

small blind. This is usually a sign of a weak player who's hoping to get lucky on the flop. If he doesn't hit the flop, he'll surely be forced out by a player who bets the flop aggressively. Against late position raises, consider playing more aggressively before the flop. For example, if the button raises and you think he's trying to steal the blinds, reraise him with a hand such as A-10.

Playing from the small blind is even tougher when going heads-up against the big blind. With only one blind left in the hand, some would argue that an aggressive raise with a marginal hand makes sense. After all, there's only one player that could call your bluff.

I disagree completely with this approach. Instead of raising from the small blind, simply call with marginal to good hands, and fold your garbage cards.

Solid players understand the power of position. They look to minimize the pot size (as well as their losses) rather than build a large pot where they may be forced to make difficult post-flop decisions. With premium hands—K-K, A-K, or even J-J—raising from the small blind works because your hand is strong enough to warrant playing a bigger pot.

Another problem with raising with weak hands from the small blind is that most players will defend their big blind with a wide variety of cards. That makes it extremely hard to get a read on your opponent's hand after the flop. Unless you catch a good flop, you'll often be waving the white flag, declaring "Okay, take it. I missed."

Let's take a hand like A♦ 6♣. It rates to be stronger than a random big blind hand, but when you factor in post-flop betting, even an 8-9 in the big blind can crush you in the long run. When you catch an ace on the flop, you'll likely get no action. If you do get action, there's a good chance your opponent has you beat. If you miss the flop and bet anyway, your opponent can take down the pot with a raise. Even if he calls on a flop such as 10-7-3, you'd have to be concerned.

Playing the small blind is no fun, but that's just the way it is. Don't lose more chips than you have to by laughing in the face of position.

22

Defending Your Big Blind: Should You or Shouldn't You?

Playing hands from the big blind can be tricky. On one side of the coin, you're in bad position because you'll have to act early, if not first, in all future betting rounds. On the other side, you've already invested money in the pot.

Let's look at a $10/$20 limit Texas hold'em game scenario. In the big blind, you hold 7-8 offsuit. A player in middle position raises the pot, the small blind folds, and now just you and the raiser are left in the hand. Sure, 7-8 isn't a very strong hand, and you wouldn't play it from an early position outside the blinds, but should you call with this hand if you've already invested a bet?

Take a look at the math.

Your opponent has thrown $20 in the pot. In addition, there's $5 from the small blind, plus the $10 you've already put in. That adds up to $35. It only costs you $10 to call. You're getting odds of 3.5 to 1, and you only have one player to beat.

It's clear that 7-8 offsuit isn't going to be a favorite over most of the hands your opponent will raise with, but since you're getting such favorable odds, it doesn't have to be. Consider that if your opponent raised with A-K, your 7-8 still has a 38 percent chance to win the pot.

Making the call is a reasonable play.

In a no-limit hold'em tournament, it really gets interesting, especially when antes are added to the mix. Once again, you're in the big blind. This time your hand is 6-4 offsuit. There are nine players at the table who have anted $100 each, and the blinds are $400/$800. Right off the bat, there's $2,100 in the pot.

A tight player, representing a strong hand, raises the minimum under the gun. Everyone folds to you, and you're faced with the prospect of putting $800 in to call. With his $1,600 raise, the pot now totals $3,700.

You only have to call $800 more to win $3,700, giving you close to 5 to 1 odds. Even if your opponent shows you that he has pocket aces you'd still want to call this bet; pocket rockets are only slightly better than a 4 to 1 favorite against 6-4 offsuit.

There are some drawbacks, however, to defending your blind with trash hands. When you start with garbage out of position, you might find yourself forced to make very difficult decisions. For example, if the flop comes 9-6-2, should you bet with your 6-4? Should you check and then fold to a bet? What about a check-raise?

Playing optimal poker isn't easy. The very best players in the world—those who consistently make correct decisions in sticky situations—are generally known as tough blind defenders. Without doubt they do the math, but they're also very confident in their ability to read opponents and strategically bluff them out. Ideally, that should be your goal as well.

You need to learn to defend your big blind, but it's not a strategy that a beginner can master immediately. As a novice, you'd be better off folding some of your big blind garbage so you won't make costly mistakes later in the hand. Even the best professionals won't defend a big blind with 7-2 offsuit.

By defending your big blind more often and contesting more pots, you'll send a message to the rest of the table that your big blind is not for sale. That table presence really works.

Incidentally, if you know that a certain player in the big blind will only call a raise with a very strong hand, never give him a break. Apply maximum pressure on him. However, if a big blind player sometimes reraises, or calls most of the time, give him a little respect. Instead of raising his big blind at will, be more selective against him. Go after easier targets instead.

23

Fancy Play Syndrome

Fancy Play Syndrome is a phrase first coined by renowned poker author Mike Caro. FPS, as it often is called, is a disease that many poker players suffer from today, and it often causes severe damage to the wallets of the afflicted.

Symptoms of this horrible malady include checking when you should bet, raising in bizarre situations, calling when you should be raising, and raising when you should be folding.

Here's a little quiz to test whether you suffer from FPS.

Do you call in situations where the correct play is a raise?

I've often seen players trying to be too cute when pots gets large, thus risking the entire pot in the hopes of squeezing out a few extra bucks from their opponents. Unfortunately, what often happens is they just end up losing the hand.

Here's a simple example. The FPS sufferer holds K-Q, and the board reads J♠ 10♠ 9♥ 4♥. The pot is already extremely large, and FPS's opponent bets the pot.

FPS will often just call here, but the correct play is to protect the hand and raise big. FPS believes he can trick his opponent into thinking he has a weak hand, and hopes his opponent will make a big bet on the river. However, with the pot already large, and his hand far from invincible, he needs to make winning the pot his priority.

Do you care more about making cool plays when standard tactics make more sense?

In Texas hold'em, check-raising an opponent three times in the same hand is akin to a 5' 8" defender swatting a Shaquille O'Neal dunk attempt into the crowd. It's the ultimate move to embarrass an opponent. However, this move hardly ever works. When an FPS sufferer tries it too many times, he ends up costing himself value bets that his opponents may have called.

Say the flop is A♥ 7♦ 3♥, and FPS holds the K♥ 10♥. FPS checks, his opponent bets, and FPS throws in a semibluff raise. His opponent calls.

The turn is the J♥ giving FPS the nut flush. He decides to check again. The opponent bets, and once again FPS raises. The river is a blank, the 8♠.

It's extremely unlikely that FPS's opponent will go for a check-raise again. But that doesn't stop him from trying. In this case, when a river bet might have been called by an opponent, FPS let him off the hook by trying to get too fancy with yet another check-raise.

Do you bet four of a kind on the flop thinking, "No one will figure me for that hand?"

This is a common mistake made by lots of poker players. Let's look at an example. Five people have called and the FPS victim is in the big blind with 3♥ 3♦. The flop comes 3♠ 8♦ 3♣, giving him incredible quads. While it's true that if he bets the flop his opponents likely won't figure him for four of a kind, it's still the wrong play and it will cost him money in the long run.

What would his opponents have to hold in order to call? Since he's in the big blind, they may not figure him for quads, but they certainly might put him on a set of threes, in which case, unless an opponent held 8-8, no one could beat his trips. Besides, if someone were holding 8-8, FPS would get all his money anyway.

The key reasons for checking quads are to let others try to bluff the hand, and to let players with overcards catch up. If someone holds 7-7 or 9-9, they could catch a full house on the turn, which means a smart player is in for a big payday.

If you answered yes to all three questions, you have full-blown Fancy Play Syndrome and are in serious need of help. Here's the cure: Forget the fancy stuff and focus on betting fundamentals.

If you answered yes to two questions, you're headed down the wrong path. It's time to change course.

If you answered yes to just one question, there is hope for you. In poker, creativity is a good thing, but make sure you only employ fancy plays sporadically.

If you answered no to all three questions, it's likely you're doing very well at the tables, and show none of the dreaded symptoms of FPS.

24

Dummy it Down

There's an old poker saying that goes something like this: "If thou attempts to bluff a bad player, thou becomes one." Learn what this adage means and your poker results will improve immensely. I like to call it dummying down your game.

You see, sophisticated moves are totally lost on players who aren't really paying attention, or who don't truly understand the value of their own cards. The best way to profit from these players is to play a fundamentally sound game.

Don't get cute. It's a waste of time. When you find yourself up against some very weak players, make the conscious decision to simplify your game.

I hate to say it, but even in the main event of the World Series of Poker, it's extremely important to dummy down your game. Despite the $10,000 entry fee, most participants are amateurs with very low poker skills.

Dummying down is not hard to do. Here are some key strategies.

Avoid Bluffing

Bad players call too often to make bluffing a profitable long run play. If you raise with A-K and two bad players call, don't waste any more money after the flop if you don't improve your hand. If the flop comes 8-6-3, you should be willing to check and give up if somebody bets.

Value Bet Marginal Hands

Since bad players call way too often with weak holdings, punish them for their foolishness. Bet not only when you have the strongest hands but also when you have mediocre cards that are likely to be the best hand.

Let's say the flop comes Q-10-4 and you hold A-10.

If a bad player checks to you, bet your pair of tens for value. If he calls, continue to bet the hand to the river. Don't worry too much about what he has. Unless the board becomes messy—say, with a jack and a nine—bet your hand all the way to the end and hope that your opponent makes a stupid call with a terrible hand.

Note that there is a big difference between betting a pair of 10s for value and bluffing. Despite the fact that you don't have a strong hand, you aren't bluffing. You have a hand that rates to beat a bad player, so make sure that you're paid for it in full.

Skip the Trickery

When playing against skilled opponents, you must find ways to disguise the strength of your hands. Smart players do this by betting their hands in ways that might confuse a thinking opponent.

There's no need for that strategy against a bad player. Check-raising and setting traps are pointless moves. Instead, as boring and uneventful as it may seem, simply bet your hands in a straightforward manner.

Trying to be tricky will only cost you money. For example,

let's say that you have a flush draw against a skilled opponent. You hit your flush on the river and decide to check-raise since your opponent is so aggressive. That play can work against a strong opponent, but it's doomed to fail against a beginner. Why? Because a novice will surely call if he has any sort of a hand, but he won't bet if you check first.

Winning at poker isn't flashy and glamorous. You profit by capitalizing on opponents' mistakes. That's especially true against less-skilled, less-observant and plain bad players.

So, dummy it down when facing, you know, dummies!

25

Avoiding Traps

Poker is as much about cutting your losses as it is winning pots. The ability to fold a strong hand in the right situation can save you loads of money, which essentially adds to your bottom line. Money saved is money earned.

Let's look at some trapping situations and how you can avoid them to cut your losses.

Situation #1

You raise before the flop holding A-A and two players call. The flop comes J♠ J♦ 4♣. Both players check and you bet the pot.

If even one player calls you in this situation, be wary of a possible trap; you're the intended target. If both players call, or even raise, then you should have the discipline to fold your hand, despite its apparent strength. If one of your opponents has a jack, your pocket aces are as good as pocket deuces.

Situation #2

You raise before the flop with A-Q and an opponent reraises.

While A-Q looks tempting, you have to consider what cards your opponent may have. A reraise before the flop is usually a sign of strength. It's very possible that your opponent has one of the following hands: A-A, K-K, Q-Q or A-K. Against any of these hands, an A-Q is in terrible shape. An opponent's reraise could also mean he holds J-J, 10-10, or 9-9, but A-Q is still an underdog here as well.

Even if you are lucky enough to catch an ace or a queen, a player with pocket nines isn't going to give you the action you desire when he sees an overcard to his pair on the board.

Situation #3

You raise before the flop with K-K and get three callers.

The flop comes 6♠ 8♠ 9♣ and you bet to protect your hand. If an opponent raises on a board like this one, don't rule out the real possibility that you could be drawing nearly dead. The list of hands that pocket kings do well against on a raised flop that comes down like this are few. Several hands can crush you. There's no reason to think that a player wouldn't be in there with a 7-5, or even my old favorite, 7-10. Other likely hands include 6-6, 8-8, 9-9, and 8-9.

While each one of those hands has you beat, another possibility is that an opponent is raising you with a strong draw. If so, your cowboys are only a small favorite.

If another player has 7-7, he has 10 outs to beat you. If he holds 7♠ 9♠, he has an incredible 20 outs to win the pot with two cards to come! He's a substantial statistical favorite to win.

A pair of kings, or any overpair to the board, is a strong hand. But when the flop cards are coordinated, or there's a flush draw present, danger lurks.

Situation #4

You're deep into a hand, holding the Q♥ 10♥. The flop came with the J♥ A♠ 3♥, followed by the 7♣ on the turn.

Your opponent bet on the flop and turn, and you called. On the river, you complete your flush when the 5♥ hits. Your opponent checks to you. This looks like a good opportunity to try to make a value bet. So, you do.

Then your opponent check-raises!

There are only two hands stronger than yours: a king-high flush and the ace-high flush. Both are unlikely, but if he check-raised on the river, you should only call at most. Do not reraise. A reraise here has little value, as the hands that he will most likely call with are precisely the ace-high and king-high flushes.

All of these situations will come up in a game of no-limit Texas hold'em. The next time you see one of these traps developing against you, be prepared. If not, don't say I didn't warn you.

PART III:
BETTING AND BLUFFING WITH NO FEAR

You've probably heard more than a few poker players say that learning how much to bet in no-limit hold'em is pivotal to success. Just as important is what type of action to take. That is, should you fold, just call, raise, reraise, or check-raise? Here are a few tips on how to make key betting decisions in hold'em.

26

How Much Should You Bet?

People who study Texas hold'em first learn the hands that are strong enough to play. Most poker books go into detail explaining premium hands such as A-A, K-K, Q-Q, A-K, as well as marginal starters such as 8-8, 9-9 and A-Q. However, knowing what cards to start with is only the tip of the iceberg when it comes to understanding how to effectively play no-limit hold'em. Frankly, it's the easy part.

The real trick to playing this game for profit is learning how much to bet on those hands in various situations. Knowing what cards to play won't be very useful if you continually misplay them by betting the wrong amount.

Betting the right amount is dictated by your personal skill level. A novice player should make larger bets than a professional. With blinds at $100/$200, I'd recommend that a beginner raise anywhere from $800 to $1,000 chips when he decides to play. An experienced player would be better off raising $500 to $600.

The reason is simple: A novice has a much better chance to win the pot before the flop than he does after it. A player with tons of experience would rather see a flop cheaply and make his key decisions after the flop. Let's look at an example where a professional would fare better after the flop than a novice.

Suppose the beginner holds J-J and raises to $600 before the flop. Three other players call him, and the flop comes Q-7-4. This is a situation where he can get into trouble. While the pocket jacks started out as a strong hand, the flopped queen is a danger card. If someone holds K-Q or A-Q, the jacks will be in bad shape.

So, how should you proceed?

Here's where an experienced player has the edge. He is better equipped to read his opponents and make an informed decision. If the veteran is holding the jacks, he'll likely know whether they are still strong. The beginner, though, will be in no-man's-land.

An advanced player may decide to check and see what develops. He might even make a small, feeler bet of about one-third the size of the pot. But for beginners, I recommend making a large bet to define opponents' hands. If there's $2,700 in the middle, go ahead and bet the whole pot.

Until a beginner really knows what he's doing, I advise that he make those large raises—four to five times the amount of the big blind—before the flop. His post-flop bets should be the size of the pot.

Ideally, the goal is to become experienced enough to make smaller bets. That is the most effective strategy.

What does your bet accomplish?

For those of you ready to take that next step, it's time to think about what your bet is accomplishing. Because you and your opponents will miss the flop a high percentage of the time, most of your post-flop bets should be made to obtain valuable information.

Let's say that you hold 9-9, and raise to $600. The big blind is the only caller. The flop comes A-7-4 and the big blind checks to you. Even though the ace is a huge scare card, making a bet on the flop will accomplish two things: You'll protect your hand if you're ahead, and you'll also define your opponent's hand.

A small bet of $200 simply won't give you enough information, because your opponent will call such a small bet with a wide variety of hands. But if you bet the size of the pot, $1,300 in this example, you'll definitely get the information you're looking for.

But is it necessary to risk that much? If you bet $1,100, wouldn't you get that same information? Yes, you sure would! And even less would work as well. So, make an assertive, yet careful bet, something like $900, or approximately two-thirds the size of the pot.

By betting about two-thirds of the pot instead of the entire amount, you'll save some money on your bluff attempts and still be able to define your opponent's hand. As an added bonus, you'll get extra calls when you catch a monster hand.

When Less is More

Betting less to get the same result as betting more is a relatively simple concept, especially among top tier players, but it's a strategy that many novice and average players haven't fully grasped.

Situations frequently arise in no-limit hold'em when a smaller bet will actually give you more bang for your buck. More specifically, there are times when betting half the pot will give you the same amount of information as betting the whole pot.

Let's look at another example to help clarify this point. Suppose you're playing no-limit hold'em and raised before the flop with A-10. Only the player in the big blind called you, so you continue to play heads-up with $700 in the pot.

The flop comes K♣ 8♠ 4♦. The big blind checks to you. You decide to bet in the hope that your opponent missed the flop and will fold. The question is, how much should you bet?

If you bet the whole pot, $700, you'll definitely find out if your opponent is serious about continuing with the hand. If he calls the pot-sized bet, chances are he has a better hand than your ace-high.

While we know that we can find out with a $700 bet, the pertinent questions are: Do you really need to risk the whole $700 to gather that information? Would the outcome be any different had you bet, say, $450?

Probably not. A pot-sized bet and a bet of approximately one-half the pot will yield about the same information. However, the smaller bet is often a much better choice for several reasons:

1. When you're bluffing, you'll be risking fewer chips when you get caught. When you are attempting to flat-out steal the pot, it doesn't matter whether you bet one-half, three-quarters, or even the full pot—any of these amounts will generally give you sufficient information as to whether your opponent hit the flop.

So, why risk betting the whole pot in this situation when a smaller bet will accomplish the same objective?

2. When you actually have a good hand and want your opponents to play with weaker hands, they'll be more likely to call a bet of one-half the pot rather than a full pot-sized bet. If you have a monster hand and are looking for action, betting half the pot will get you a few more loose calls, and that's exactly what you want.

3. The math is on your side. Virtually every poker situation can be broken down into a simple mathematical formula. If there is $600 in a pot and you bet $600, you'll be getting even money on your proposition. That means you'd have to win that pot just over half of the time to make it a profitable play in the long run. (There are other factors that come into play on the next two cards, but let's ignore them for this example.)

When you consider that the hand will play out almost

identically with a $400 bet, you'll see that, mathematically, it often makes sense to choose the smaller bet.

If you bet $400, you're risking $400 to win $600, meaning that you're getting 3 to 2 odds rather than even money. The smaller bet will achieve virtually the same result as the bigger bet but will only have to pay off just over 40 percent of the time rather than 50 percent of the time to make it a profitable play in the long run.

You will rarely see a top professional bet the size of the pot when you watch poker on television. They generally vary their bets between one-third, one-half, and three-quarters of the pot. They understand that by keeping the pots smaller, they'll have more control over the outcome. And that's just what they want to do—maintain control of the table.

Amateurs, however, will often make oversized bets out of fear. They worry that a superior player will be able to outplay them if they don't make a sizeable bet. Frankly, that thinking isn't too far off base.

Playing small-bet poker is for professionals and those who aspire to improve their game to a professional level. If that's not where you are, it just might make sense for you to swing for the fences.

27

Selling a Poker Hand is Like Selling a Car

The ability to sell is a core skill that you need to master in order to do well at the poker table. You see, being a great poker player is like being a successful car salesman.

When a salesman tries to sell you a Chevy, there are several tells he'll look for. This information helps him get maximum value for the sale. He'll ask you what you do for a living, how much you make, things like that. The more information he gathers, the more likely he'll be able to sell you a car at the highest price.

So, you ask, what in the world does any of this have to do with poker?

Plenty. In no-limit hold'em, the amount you bet could be the difference between getting fully paid off for your strong hand or scaring away a potential "buyer." It could mean the difference between a winning session and a losing session.

The key difference in poker, though, is that you only have one chance to get it right. A car salesman can always lower his price if it looks like the sticker is too high, but a poker player doesn't have that luxury. Therefore, it's even more important to do your "market research" and understand who the buyer is.

At the poker table, the clues you're looking for are right in front of you.

- You hold powerful cards, but how strong is your opponent's hand? The stronger you think it is, the more you should bet.

- Does your opponent think you bluff a lot? If you were caught bluffing earlier, how much did you bet then? This is important because you may now want to bet the same amount with a strong hand.

- How many chips does your opponent have? This is similar to the car salesman who asks his customer how much he makes. The fewer chips your opponent has, the more precious they are to him.

Selling your hand for maximum value is a skill that truly separates the great players from the wannabes. It takes true talent to figure out how much you can squeeze out of an opponent without scaring him off, especially since you only have one chance to get it right.

I recently did a reality show where my job was to teach Rob, of "Survivor" fame, how to become a professional poker player. In one particular session, he took home a decent win of about $400, yet I still blasted him.

Why? Because Rob could have won more from his opponents if he'd bet the right amount, but he just didn't get it. His response was, "I won, didn't I?"

Yes, but he didn't win enough. If he had played his cards right, he would have won $1,000! The way I see it, Rob lost $600. When you're a professional poker player, that's how you have to look at it.

You can teach anyone the right cards to play, the odds of this or that, and the power of position. However, the most important skill—knowing the correct amount to bet—is the most difficult to teach because it relies so heavily on your ability to sell.

There's a big difference between a bet of $1,200 and one of $1,325. If you could have won $1,325, but instead only pocketed $1,200, you just lost $125 that an expert wouldn't have lost.

Like a good car salesman, study the customer and then close the deal.

28

Smart Preflop Raises

In no-limit hold'em, a standard raise is exactly three times the amount of the big blind. So, if the blinds are $10/$20, the normal raise will make it $60 to go. This is a solid preflop raising strategy, but you should also consider adjusting the amount you raise based on several key factors.

The most important consideration is the type of opponents you're up against, especially the player whose big blind you're raising. As a rule, if the player is skilled and usually defends his big blind with a wide variety of hands, you must raise enough to define his hand.

A minimum raise won't give you any information about your opponent's strength. Also, it won't be enough to get him to fold. However, if you raise to four or five times the blind, your opponent will need a stronger hand to justify calling the raise.

On the flipside, if the big blind is a very conservative player, he won't defend his blind unless he holds premium cards. So, your raise can be smaller than normal. A raise of 2.5 times the big blind should be enough to win the hand unless someone else has strong preflop cards.

You should also consider the type of game you're in. In a tournament, you'll often find weaker players who are overly concerned with survival. This makes them play conservatively. Therefore, your raises can be somewhat smaller in tournaments than they are in cash games. Make it 2.5 times the big blind when playing in tourneys.

In a cash game, however, raise at least three times the blind. Cash-game players have much larger chip stacks in front of them and play is often looser. Your preflop raise should reflect that.

Another major factor that can't be overlooked is the presence of antes. All no-limit hold'em games are dealt with a small and big blind, but in some cases, especially in tournaments, antes are also introduced. This slightly changes the math.

In a typical tournament with blinds at $400/$800, every player will have to ante an additional $100. With nine players at your table, there's already $2,100 in the pot. Because of this, the player in the big blind will be getting very good odds to call any small raise. Your raise should be large enough to discourage that.

Many players don't pay enough attention to the antes. They play the same way when an ante is charged as they did when there was no ante. If that's the case, continue to make your raises 2.5 times the blind. Let's say you make it $2,000 to go at the $400/$800 plus $100-ante level. If everyone folds, you'll be risking $2,000 to win $2,100. That's much better than risking $2,000 to win only $1,200 when no antes are present.

The last key factor is position. Make larger preflop raises when you're out of position. This gives you the opportunity to win the hand right there rather than playing it out of position after the flop. So, if you plan to raise from the small blind, make it a very large raise. A big raise forces opponents to call a significant amount if they intend to try to outmaneuver you post-flop.

29

Coming Over the Top

You've probably heard the axiom, "Poker isn't about the cards; it's about reading people." True. Here's a tip that illustrates how you can apply people-reading skills to a poker hand, regardless of what you hold. Every top professional poker player out there uses this valuable no-limit hold'em play.

The play is a preflop reraise, otherwise known as "coming over the top."

For example, you're playing in a no-limit hold'em tournament, and the blinds are $100/$200 with a $25 ante. A loose player raises to $600 from middle position. Everyone folds to you, sitting on the dealer button with Q-3 offsuit.

This would seem to be an obvious folding situation, but it's not necessarily so. If you have a read on your opponent and you have a conservative table image, you might easily take this pot down by coming over the top with a reraise. Including the loose player's initial raise, there is $1,125 in the pot (blinds $300, antes $225 and initial raise $600). If you reraise the bet to $2,600, chances are good that both blinds will fold—unless one of them picks up a powerful hand such as A-A or K-K, but that would be unlikely.

Then the action returns to Mr. Loose. Unless you were wrong about your initial read, and he does hold a strong hand, he'll fold. More times than not, your investment of $2,600 will win you $1,125, and none of that has anything to do with the strength of your hand. Basically, you're laying odds of a little more than 2 to 1 that your raise will win the pot right there.

But what do you do if the guy calls? That's the tricky part. If he calls, you need to slam on the brakes. Coming over the top works best before the flop, not after it.

Since your opponent decided to look you up, the pro's way of saying call, you must realize that he has a very strong hand. Now, you might take just one more shot at the pot on the flop. However, if he calls again, proceed only if you hit a miracle flop yourself.

The play works even better with more players in the hand. Here's why. Let's say the initial situation is the same: Mr. Loose makes it $600 to go, but this time, a player behind him calls. You have 2-7 offsuit, the worst hand in poker. There is already $1,725 in the pot. Your raise will be about the same, say $2,600. This time you're risking $2,600 to win $1,725, a much better return.

The second player who called actually helps you in two ways. First, you know it's unlikely that he can call your reraise, because if he had a strong hand such as A-A or K-K, he probably would have reraised himself. Second, he makes your raise look even more legitimate, since you've represented power by reraising two people.

Because over-the-top plays are designed for preflop wins, you don't want to use this tactic on hands that have strong post-flop potential. Hands like 7-7 or 7♠ 8♠ actually want to see a cheap flop; you're hoping to flop a set or hit a straight or flush. Just call in these situations and save your over-the-top plays for trash hands like Q-4, A-6, or even 7-2.

Here's another benefit of the over-the-top play: It helps to strengthen your table image. I hear players complain all the time that they never catch a hand, or that they have bad luck. Reraise over the top and you'll manufacture a hand and make your own luck.

Adding this play to your repertoire will help increase your chip count with very little risk. It also adds texture to your game. Once your opponents catch on to the fact that you're willing to come over the top, you'll get the action you want when you're dealt power hands such as A-A or K-K.

30

Calling is Cool

It drives me batty when I watch poker on television and hear commentators say things like, "Well, this looks like a raise or fold situation. He certainly can't call." I disagree with their assessment a good eight out of ten times.

It's not only TV commentators who get this wrong, but many poker book authors as well. I won't name names (because I have to work with these people!), but the truth is, there's plenty of literature out there that incorrectly advises risky post-flop play.

Frankly, that raise-or-fold mentality is a little too kamikaze for my taste.

Calling is a powerful weapon when used correctly. While it's not as sexy as a big all-in move, it's a safer, more controlled way to play certain situations in no-limit hold'em tournaments.

You'll often hear that in order to win a poker tournament you have to play aggressively. That's true, but what does "aggressively" actually mean?

Professionals play aggressively by entering many hands and taking a few more stabs at the pot than their opponents do. Pros don't make dangerous raises in marginal situations where they unnecessarily risk a high percentage of their chips. In other words, pros call when it is the best play.

Let's look at an example where calling is not only safer, but often the better play.

Suppose you have A-A and raise before the flop. The player in the big blind is the only caller. The flop comes K♦ 4♠ 4♣. If your opponent bets the flop, what would you do? You have a powerful hand here, but if your opponent happens to have trip fours, you're dead meat. The only way you'll win the pot against his trip fours is by catching one of the two remaining aces, and that's not likely.

On the other hand, your opponent may hold something like K-Q, giving him two smaller pair than yours. If that's the case, you're in excellent shape. He could only beat you if he catches one of the remaining two kings. Even better, your opponent might have nothing at all and is just trying to buy the pot.

This is definitely not a raise or fold situation. In fact, the absolute best play here is to call. I can prove it.

If your opponent is bluffing and you raise him, you'll cost yourself any further action on the hand if he had intended to continue to bluff. Instead, he'll probably fold. If your opponent has you beat, raising could cost you more chips than necessary. By just calling him down to the river, you protect yourself from losing more than you should.

If your opponent has the king, chances are he'll bet the hand for you all the way to fifth street. However, if he happens to check on the turn or river, you can then take over the betting.

One of the undeniable keys to winning a no-limit tournament is manipulating the pot size. Naturally, this is much easier to do when you have position. By calling your opponent down, you're able to maintain position with little risk, and keep him in the dark as to the strength of your hand.

There are many other situations where calling on the flop

is a better option than raising. Let's look at one more. Suppose your opponent raises before the flop, and you call with J-J. The flop comes Q♦ 10♠ 4♥. Your opponent bets.

If you raise here to define your opponent's hand, it'll be expensive. The cheaper route is to flat call on the flop. Then, if your opponent bets again on the turn, it's highly likely that your jacks are beaten. You can now fold without wasting a raise on the flop.

Conserving your chips by losing the minimum on a hand is nearly as good as winning a pot. The chips you save by calling instead of raising will allow you to see more flops and win more pots down the road.

31

Calling With Nothing

"Calling with nothing" is a strategy that nearly every top professional on the poker circuit uses. This play is one of the best methods to increase your stack size in tournaments without risking too many of your chips.

For this play to work, one thing is imperative: You must have position on your opponent. For example, say that your adversary is in the small blind and you're in the big blind. You'll have position throughout the hand; it could be the perfect time to employ this little trick.

Let's look at an example of how this play works. You're playing in a no-limit Texas hold'em tournament and the blinds are at $200/$400 with a $50 ante. With nine players at the table, the pot adds up to $1,050 before the cards are even dealt.

Everyone folds to the small blind, and he raises the bet to a total of $1,200. In this situation, you should call with a wide variety of hands.

Here's why. It only costs you $800 more to call, and there's already $2,050 in the pot. You're getting over 2.5 to 1 odds on the call. Your opponent doesn't necessarily have to have a very strong hand—he could very well be trying to steal the pot. He may hold cards such as A-6, K-10, or even 4-4.

After you call, there is $2,850 in the pot, and you're in great position. The goal now is to either flop a good hand, or hope that your opponent misses the flop so that you can steal the pot from him.

Let's say that you're holding J-9. The flop comes down 4♥ 5♥ 7♣. If your opponent bets something like $1,500, you can call again. Why? He may be making a continuation bet. In other words, since he raised before the flop, he might be attempting another stab at the pot with virtually any hand.

When you call his bet this time, though, it should freeze him if he missed the flop. After all, your call on the flop makes it appear as though you have something that connected with the board.

The turn is the key time to capitalize on this ploy. That's when you can spring into action and take control of the hand. However, if your opponent bets the turn in front of you, your strategy won't work as well. If a player raises preflop, bets the flop, and then bets the turn, it's likely that he has improved his hand, or really did start with a strong pair.

Suppose, though, that the turn card is a 6, so that the board reads 4-5-6-7. Even if your opponent has pocket aces, you should still be able to win this pot with a bet. The only time you'll run into trouble is when your opponent raised with a hand such as A-8 suited. Since you have played your hand so passively up to this point, there's no reason for your opponent to think that you're bluffing the straight.

If he doesn't have the straight himself, he'll probably check to you. When he does, it's your turn to pounce. You should bet an amount between 50 percent and 75 percent of the pot.

If your opponent check-raises you on the turn, it's time to abort mission and take your lumps. If he just calls your bet, it's probably wise to shut down on the river, unless you think he may be drawing to a flush and a third flush card doesn't come.

People often tell me that they never seem to get enough premium hands to build a big stack of chips. Perhaps now you understand better how the pros seem to do it on a regular basis. It isn't that they get better cards than you do—it's just that they have a few extra tricks up their sleeve.

32

Calling with the Worst Hand

Situations will sometimes arise at the poker table when you just know that your opponent has you beat, but you should call anyway. A perfect example occurred recently on NBC's National Heads-Up Poker Championship in a hand between me and my good friend, poker professional, Evelyn Ng.

Evelyn

Daniel

Flop

Evelyn raised to $1,200 before the flop, and I called with the J♠ 9♠. The flop came J♦ 4♥ 3♦. I checked to Evelyn and she bet $1,600. At that point, she was ahead in the match, and I only had $12,600 in chips left.

After much thought, I finally decided to go all-in hoping that she couldn't beat my pair of jacks. She thought about calling for quite some time, but eventually folded the 7♦ 4♦. On the surface, it might seem like Evelyn made the right decision. After all, I had a pair of jacks and she only had a pair of fours. However, in poker, there is often more to it than hand strength alone.

First, let's look at the odds of her hand against mine.

Since she could catch a 4, a 7, or a diamond to win the pot, her hand was actually the slight favorite at 51 percent. In fact, the only hands that she wouldn't be favored against would be two pair or three of a kind. Even against trip jacks, she would still win the pot almost 30 percent of the time.

That's not the only thing she had to ponder.

Evelyn was faced with a bet of $11,000, but with the chips that had already been put in before the flop, as well as the bet she made on the flop, she would have to risk $11,000 to win $16,600. She was even money to win the pot, but the pot was laying her approximately 3 to 2 odds ($16,600/$11,000). Also, she had to consider that she had an opportunity to end the match if her hand was better than mine.

Note that certain draws are *so* powerful that they can actually be the favorite to win the pot. For example, if you hold the 5♥ 6♥ and the flop comes 6♦ 7♥ 8♥, you're the favorite to win the pot—even against pocket aces! In fact, you're a substantial favorite, improving to become the winning hand about 64 percent of the time.

You can use the following rule to help figure out whether or not your drawing hand is a favorite against an opponent: After the flop, if there are 13 cards that will improve your hand to the winner, then you're a very small underdog. If 14 cards can make your hand, you'll be just about even money to win. With 15 or more outs, you're the favorite.

Here's a hand example I recently analyzed.

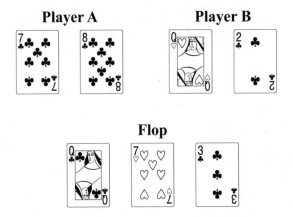

Player A   Player B

Flop

Player A has 13 cards to improve his hand (eight clubs, two sevens, and three eights). His hand will win the pot 47 percent of the time.

Now, change the deuce in Player B's hand from the 2♣ to the 2♥, and Player A actually goes from an underdog to being a very slight favorite, winning the pot 50.1 percent of the time. Even more enticing, in a hand where Player A has 15 outs, he'd be more than a 56 percent favorite.

You don't need a degree in mathematics to play poker, but it will serve you well to remember these odds.

This knowledge becomes increasingly important when playing in no-limit hold'em tournaments. An extreme example is a situation where a player has gone all in, and you're the big blind with a pitiful hand like 2-3 offsuit.

You know for certain that your opponent has you beat, but that doesn't necessarily mean that you should fold. First, calculate the pot odds you're getting. Then, assess your chances of winning by counting your outs.

Here's a final example: You have $400 in the big blind, and an opponent goes all in for $700. So, the bet facing you is only $300 more. Including the small blind, you'd be risking $300 to win $1,300. That's over 4 to 1 pot odds and is very favorable. Even if your opponent has a powerful hand such as A-K, you'd still get lucky and win the pot 34 percent of the time.

You won't win at poker by simply playing good hands. In order to reach that next level, you need to change the way you think about the game. Don't always be concerned with whether or not you have the best cards. Instead, focus on whether or not the pot odds dictate that you should play the hand.

33

The Continuation Bet

There's a myth among no-limit Texas hold'em players that goes like this: If you raise before the flop, then you must continue to bet on the flop. Yes, in limit hold'em you should bet the flop a high percentage of the time if you raised before the flop, regardless of what comes. In no-limit, however, you should be a little more cautious with your continuation bets.

For example, let's say you're in a no-limit tournament with the blinds at $50/$100. Holding the A♣ K♠, you make it $250 to go. The player on the button calls, as does the player in the small blind.

The flop comes Q♥ 10♠ 9♦. The player in the small blind checks. What would you do? If you believe the myth, you'd probably bet about $600. However, that's not the move I'd make.

While you have a nice starting hand, and might even catch a jack for the nut straight, you have to consider what types of hands your two opponents could have. Commonly played hands they might call your raise with include K-J, 10-J, A-Q, 9-9, K-Q, A-10, and 6-6.

Most of those hands, with the exception of the sixes, are

substantial favorites over yours. If both of your opponents have small pairs, which they probably don't, then your continuation bet might work. It's also unlikely that both of your opponents completely missed this coordinated board.

Keep this in mind: Saving bets at the poker table is just as good as earning bets.

Money you don't lose is money that stays in your stack. Making an automatic bet after the flop in a situation where it's highly likely that one, or both, of your opponents will call, is a play that will lose you money in the long run.

In this example, if you check the flop, you give yourself a free chance to catch up—provided the button doesn't bet. By betting, you not only cost yourself money, but also open up the possibility that the small blind could check-raise.

If you've studied your opponents for a while, you'll pick up patterns in their play. At the very least, you'll know what types of hands they play before the flop. That information will help you decide when it looks safe to make continuation bets.

Let's look at another hand. You raise preflop with the Q♥ J♥, and the player seated next to you calls. The flop is 2♠ 2♦ 3♣.

What you've learned about your opponent is that he wouldn't call your raise with small cards like those, so you feel safe in thinking that he didn't catch any of that flop. You also know that he usually reraises before the flop when he has a pocket pair. Since he didn't reraise, chances are that he has a hand such as A-Q. If you make a continuation bet in this situation, your success rate on the bluff should be fairly high.

The real lesson is that money saved is money earned. In limit hold'em, betting the flop only costs you one unit, but in no-limit, several failed continuation bets will add up to a significant amount of money.

Plugging that hole in your game will help you avoid sloughing off chips unnecessarily.

34

When to Bet and When to Check-Raise

I often discuss the importance of mixing up your play in order to remain unpredictable. One of the best ways to do that is by occasionally betting the flop and sometimes going for a check-raise. When deciding which play makes the most sense, there are several factors to consider.

The Strength of Your Hand

The most important factor in deciding whether to bet the flop or wait for a check-raise is the power of your hand. Ask yourself this question: Could the next card cause me to lose the hand?

As a rule, if a hand is vulnerable to getting outdrawn, you should lean toward betting rather than waiting. Check-raising won't work if opponents don't bet the flop.

For example, if you hold K-K and the flop is K♥ 8♦ 3♠, there's little risk of being outdrawn on the next card; checking would be a fine play. However, if the flop is 9♦ 10♦ 3♥, consider betting now, as this board presents a dangerous situation for your hand. Your opponent could have a flush or straight draw, and even an A-10 would have five outs to beat you.

Your Opponent's Behavior

If you're planning to check-raise, you must gauge the likelihood that an opponent will bet on the flop. Timid players won't bet unless they have a strong hand. You really shouldn't check-raise them unless, of course, you have a monster hand yourself. Aggressive players, however, look to attack pots and pounce on weakness. You should check-raise them often to neutralize their bullying style.

Past History with an Opponent

Having a good memory of past hands is a great asset at the poker table. You can tap into that memory to help decide how to proceed with a hand. If your opponent picks up that you check-raise with strong hands, but bets right out with weaker hands, then consider throwing him a curveball by doing the opposite of what he expects.

Or don't. Your opponent may expect you to do the opposite, so you might even want to play it straightforward. Deception: That's the beauty of poker.

Stack Size

If you get to the point where you don't have many chips in front of you, you might as well be the one to bet the flop rather than check-raise.

The only time a small stack would go for the check-raise is when you have a monster hand and think your opponent might bet as a bluff, but likely wouldn't call your bet.

Not only is your chip count a consideration, so is the stack size of your opponent. If he's short-stacked and almost all in, going for a big payday with a check-raise offers much less value.

Table Position and the Number of Players in the Pot

This is an extremely important point. Obviously, the more players left to act behind you, the more likely it is that one of them will bet. So, if you're in the small blind with a powerful hand, and five players are sitting behind you, checking is a smart move. One of those players will likely take a stab at the pot. Then you can pounce with a raise.

However, if you have that same hand but are the second to last player to act, going for a check-raise would be extremely risky. You'd be counting on the last player to bet. If he doesn't, all your opponents get a free shot to beat you on the next card.

35

Betting Marginal Hands on the River

There are lots of things to think about in each hold'em hand: bet size, pot odds, whether to bluff, and more. One of the biggest decisions you'll be forced to make is whether or not to value bet a marginal hand, or just check it and take what's already in the middle.

A *value bet* is a bet that you make in the hope that you will get called and fully paid off for your hand.

I see a lot of novice players make the mistake of betting hands on the river that will only get called by a player who has them beat. This is called a negative EV (Expected Value) play. For example, let's say that you're dealt a strong starting hand like Q-Q, but the final board reads A♠ K♠ 10♠ 9♦ 8♣. Your opponent checks to you on the river. You decide that your queens are the best hand, and bet half the pot.

Here's the problem with your bet. At this point, you don't know what an opponent would call your bet with. If he has an ace, or even a pair of kings, he might call you. He'd at least call with a straight, and would probably check-raise you if he made the flush. So, in this situation, it's almost a certainty that an opponent's call means that you will lose the pot.

Why bet? You shouldn't—and that's my point.

Unless you're making the bet as a bluff in the hope of forcing your opponent to fold a better hand, betting your queens would be a terrible play. This isn't the time to make a value bet: There is no value!

Let's look at a slightly different situation. This time you have J-J and the flop is Q♥ 3♥ 2♠. Your opponent checks the flop and you bet. The turn card comes 10♠. Once again, your opponent checks and you bet. Now, the river card comes 4♥, and your opponent checks once more.

Even if you think that your jacks are the best hand, you should check. Your opponent could have the pair of queens, and if not, could be looking to check-raise you if he made a flush or caught a straight on the river. Here again is a scenario where you have to assess the value in betting by asking yourself, "What types of hands would this opponent call with?"

There just aren't too many hands an opponent will call you with that you can beat. In this spot, you'd be much better off protecting what's in the middle by merely checking.

Here's another example. What if you're up against an advanced player who check-raises you on the river? You'll probably have to fold. If he put you on a marginal hand, he likely viewed your bet as an opportunity to take the pot, or maybe even steal it.

Don't give him that chance. Protect what's already in the middle. This is especially true if you're playing in a no-limit tournament versus a live cash game. In tournament poker, it's almost always more important to simply win the pot. In cash games, you want to get full value for your hand.

It may sound like I'm suggesting that you should only bet the river when you have the absolute nut hand. That's not the case. Just make certain that before making any river bet, you ask yourself the following questions:

1. What are the chances that I have the best hand?

2. What does my opponent likely have, and what are the odds that he would call a bet?

3. What are the chances that my opponent is setting a trap for me and is planning to check-raise?

Ask these three questions each and every time you find yourself at the river with a marginal hand. Your answers will go a long way to making sure that your value bets actually have some value.

36

Five Ways to Spot a Bluff

Bluffing is a big part of no-limit poker, but just as important is the ability to sniff out an opponent's bluff. Here are a few things you should focus on.

1. Know your opponents

Before you even play a hand against an opponent, pay close attention to his tendencies. You must try to figure out if bluffing is a ploy that's part of his arsenal.

Being a poker player is much like being a criminal profiler. Before you make a decision about how to play your hand, try to classify your opponent as a habitual bluffer, a straightforward player, or a player who bluffs sporadically (the toughest opponent to face).

2. Look for physical tells

The most dramatic way to spot a bluff is to look your opponent in the eye and attempt to sense his fear. If he looks nervous, it could be a sign that he's bluffing.

The best method to detect an opponent's physical tells is

to simply look for anything unusual or uncharacteristic in his behavior. For example, if your opponent bets, and then suddenly puts his hand over his mouth—something he doesn't normally do—that could be a sign that he's bluffing.

On the other hand, he could just be self-conscious about his bad breath. What can I say? Reading physical tells is an inexact science.

3. Observe an opponent's bluffing style

When a player is losing, he's more likely to steam or go on tilt. He may become impatient and bluff more than usual. If you think he's steaming, be on the lookout for this type of erratic play. Keep this in mind: Some players bluff for the opposite reason. They bluff because they're bored.

Winning players, flush with confidence, often try to add deception to their game with a well-timed bluff. Others use their conservative table image to set up bluffs. For example, a very tight player might set up the table by making an effective bluff that his opponents just won't see coming. Be on the lookout for this type of player and you won't be fooled when the time comes to pick off his bluff.

4. Watch out for nuts-or-nothing players

You'll often find yourself in a hand where, based on an opponent's betting, you'll conclude that he either has the best possible hand or absolutely nothing at all. Since making the nut hand is so uncommon, you should lean toward calling a bet when you're in this situation.

5. Note strange betting patterns

This is probably the best and most accurate way to sniff out a bluff. You really need to pay attention to the way your opponent played his hands in the past in order to make educated decisions in the present. Try to spot his betting patterns. If you can, it will be easier to recognize bets that don't seem to make much sense.

For example, let's say that you've picked up the following pattern: When your opponent makes a flush on the turn, he always slowplays the hand, hoping you'll bet so that he can check-raise.

Now the flop comes K♥ 10♠ 7♥ and the turn card is the 5♥. Your opponent checked and then called on the flop, but this time he bets on the turn when the third heart hits.

Since you've figured out his betting pattern, you've probably ruled out the possibility that he has made the flush. Then again, he just may be good at mixing up his play. This is poker, after all!

37

Pros Don't Bluff As Much As You Think

The ability to bluff your opponents with a poker face might seem a little fanciful, but bluffing isn't really the way professional poker players make a living. In fact, one of the biggest mistakes amateur players make, when playing against professionals, is thinking that the pros are pulling Jedi mind tricks on them when making bluffs.

The truth is that pros win consistently, not because of bluffing tricks, but because they play with solid fundamentals and are able to recognize dangerous situations. They lose the minimum on a bad hand where an amateur may lose his entire stack.

If you've watched poker on television, you know what I'm talking about. I can't tell you how many times I've seen an amateur call a huge bet on the river with a meager hand just hoping that a pro is trying some elaborate bluff. Almost without fail, the pro will turn over a superior hand, and the amateur is left wondering why he called such a big bet with a lousy pair of deuces when the board read Q-9-8-6-4.

This was one of the most important epiphanies I've ever experienced in poker. When I first started playing in Vegas, against the likes of poker legends Johnny Chan and Doyle Brunson, I was in awe of them. It seemed they had some sort of supernatural power, that they could "see through my soul" and bluff me at will.

After getting my feet a little bit wet, though, I realized that while they were obviously great players, they couldn't see through my soul at all. They were not supernatural beings! What made them better was that they simply made fewer fundamental errors than their opponents did.

It wasn't magic. Their years of experience showed in their ability to get away from trap hands, to make good value bets, and to play the right cards in the right situations. Their success wasn't based on taking huge risks on monster bluffs.

And that's why they're still top players today.

Here's a piece of advice that should help you immensely should you ever play in a tournament against any of today's top professionals: When a pro puts all of his money on the line into one pot, he'll usually have the absolute nuts, the best possible hand.

"Wait," you're saying, "I've seen plenty of pros make huge bluffs."

Yes, pros take risks, but they do it differently. Most of them look to make tiny bluffs in smaller pots. The strategy is known as chopping away. A player who chops away will play many small pots and be aggressive in them. His aim is to steadily increase his stack size with little risk, rather than getting involved in too many marginal situations for big money.

It's similar to a boxer who's throwing lots of jabs, while at the same time keeping his guard up. He's being patient, waiting for an opening so that he can score the knockout punch. It's the same way in poker.

Here's the bottom line: When a pro plays a big pot, he'll rarely be bluffing, especially in a tournament where one misplay can cost him all of his chips.

As your game improves, your approach should mimic the professionals. When you decide to play a monster pot, make sure you have the nuts or pretty close to it. Leave the foolish gambling to the suckers!

38

Trust Your First Instinct

This tip may wind up being the most valuable one I could ever share with you. It's simple but extremely effective and powerful.

You'll often find yourself in a poker situation where it comes down to this basic question: Does he have it, or is he bluffing? All the cards are dealt, your opponent has made a bet on the river, and you hold a marginal hand that can beat a bluff but can't beat a legitimate hand.

Here's a hold'em hand that illustrates this scenario. Let's say the final board looks like this: J♠ 8♣ 4♠ 4♥ 6♣. You hold 8-9. If your opponent isn't bluffing, he surely has your pair of eights beat. Otherwise, he may have anything from a pair of jacks to a full house. If so, you're beat.

It all comes down to a read. In these situations, a player will usually go over the hand in his head and ask himself some important questions:

1. How often does this opponent bluff?

2. If he has a strong hand, would he play it the way he did?

3. Could he have a busted drawing hand, and if so, would he try to bluff with his missed draw?

4. Does he think I'm on a draw and he's trying to steal the pot?

5. Does he look like he's bluffing?

Take the time to go over a similar list of questions and you'll often find a definitive answer as to whether or not you should call your opponent's bet. For our sample hand, if you answered the questions like this—1) rarely; 2) yes; 3) not likely; 4) maybe; and 5) no—it adds up to an easy fold.

It's not always going to be that easy, though. Sometimes, you'll go through a list of questions and still have no idea what to do. I've been in this spot many times.

So what should you do in these situations?

Go with your first instinct. Think back to the very first thought that came to you about the hand, and go with it. That first instinct comes from the most powerful computer in the world, your subconscious mind. The subconscious acts as a processor, collecting data and storing it away for later use.

Have you ever been in a poker hand and somehow just *felt* like a player was bluffing? You can't explain why, really, but something tells you that you need to make the call.

That's not magic at all. Your brain is subconsciously sending a message based on all the data it has compiled. It has seen this situation pop up many times before, and, while you aren't necessarily consciously aware of it, this vital information gets stored deep in your subconscious. Malcolm Gladwell has written a fascinating book that deals with this subject. It's titled, *Blink: The Power of Thinking Without Thinking*. In it, Gladwell explains how it's often better to trust your subconscious rather than the conclusions that your conscious mind comes to.

But let's get back to poker. Your instincts tell you that an opponent is bluffing. Your conscious mind might attempt to disprove that conclusion with these kinds of thoughts: "The bet is too big. I don't want to look foolish making this loose call.

Why would he try to bluff me?"

If you only approach poker hands analytically, going over the pot odds and calculating the chances of your opponent having a certain hand, you may miss an important message being delivered to you from your subconscious. It's often described as *feel*, and all of the truly great poker players have it. You can too.

The more often you trust your subconscious, the better you'll get at reading people. As in life, practice makes perfect.

When making poker decisions, be sure to review the facts of the hand. Backtrack the betting, analyze an opponent's past behavior and current emotional state, and figure out the math. Do everything you can to solve the puzzle on your own.

But if all else fails, it's time to rely on your first instinct.

PART IV:
WHAT'S THE BEST PLAY? USING POKER WISDOM AS YOUR GUIDE

When someone asks me how I would play a particular hand, I start off by saying, "It all depends." That's because, when you've played poker for as many years as I have, you realize that there is always more than one way to play a hand. It all depends on your opponents, your position at the table, how many chips you have, the quality of your hole cards, and so on. In this section, I'll set up a few hold'em situations, and show you how the pros figure out the best way to play the hand.

39

Playing Garbage on the Button

I'm going to set up a no-limit hold'em tournament scenario, and your job is to figure out the best play. After you've made your guess, I'll reveal the answer along with the reasoning behind it.

You're in a $10,000 buy-in World Poker Tour event; first prize is over $1 million. Midway through the tournament, you're doing very well with $146,000 in chips, which puts you among the chip leaders. The blinds are at $400/$800, there's a $100 ante, and you're at a nine-handed table.

A player with $44,000 in chips raises to $2,200 from middle position. Based on your knowledge of this opponent, you don't think he has a very strong hand. The player next to him, with $38,000, calls the raise. You're on the button and have been dealt the Q♣ 3♥. You've been at the table with these players for several hours and have reraised only once all day. When you did, you held the absolute nuts, pocket aces, and you showed the table your hand.

So here's the question: What is the best play in this situation? Do you fold, call, raise $5,000 more, raise $10,000 more, or go all in?

I hope none of you chose to call or go all in.

Those two choices would be the absolute worst options. Q-3 is a garbage hand and doesn't play well after the flop. Calling with it is the worst play, closely followed by going all in.

So that leaves three legitimate options: fold, raise $5,000 more, or raise $10,000 more.

The worst of those three plays is to raise $5,000. The problem with this play is that if one of your opponents has a hand such as 7-7, he might call to see the flop. You don't want that! Since you're on a complete bluff, you want them all to fold immediately.

So it's either fold or raise $10,000 more. Folding is the safer play, but it's not the best option in this situation.

The best play here is to go for the steal by making a large reraise of $10,000 more. Now, that may seem contrary to much of what I usually preach, but this is a very specific situation where you can use your table image to your advantage.

Okay, let's get back to the hand.

There's already $6,500 in the pot and, based on your read of the situation, it's likely that the first player has a marginal hand and will fold. Since the second player just called the initial raise, he probably doesn't have a hand strong enough to call your raise either. If your read is correct, and because you've established the right table image, your success rate with this play will be very high.

Of course, the play tanks if one of the blinds picks up a big hand, or if one of the players already in the pot calls. But in the long run, investing $12,200 to win $6,500 will turn you a profit.

Here's another reason why this play works: As one of the chip leaders, a $12,200 hit won't do too much damage to your stack. Then again, you might ask yourself, why do I need $6,500 so badly if I already have close to $150,000 in chips?

One of the luxuries of having a big stack is that you can play more aggressively and accumulate even more chips with little risk. That's what winners do, and it's the mindset you need when you fork over $10,000 to play in one of these big tournaments.

Folding is the safe play, but keep in mind what Mike McDermott said in *Rounders*: "You can't lose what you don't put in the middle. But you can't win much either."

40

Flopping a Set in Texas Hold'em

A pair in the hole, whether it's 2-2 or A-A, presents a fantastic opportunity if you're lucky enough to flop three of a kind, otherwise known as a set. When you flop three of a kind, it is rare that someone else in the pot will have you beat. Quite often, though, your opponents will catch their straights or flushes on the draw and crush your trips.

While flopping a set is very fortunate, you must protect your hand, while at the same time getting maximum value for it. This presents a dilemma: How do you bet the hand?

Here are a few key pointers that will help you decide whether it's better to bet aggressively, or to sit back and let your opponents bet for you.

Flop Texture

This is probably the most important variable when deciding how to play a set. For example, if you're dealt K-K and the flop comes K♣ 7♦ 2♠, check the flop and give your opponents a chance to catch up a little bit. Since you hold pocket cowboys, the flop gives you the obvious lead. The hands you can trap are A-A, or the smaller sets of sevens or deuces. Best of all, if your opponents have any of those hands, you'll likely get all of their chips.

But what if there's a textured flop such as Q♥ 10♠ 8♥, and you have 10-10? This is what's known as an *action flop*. There's a three-card straight on board as well as a flush draw. The only hands that can beat you at this point are J-9 or Q-Q, but keep in mind, there are several hands that could draw out on you.

A player holding K-J, for example, could beat you if he catches an ace or a 9 to fill his straight. Someone else holding the A♥ J♥ could win with a heart, a 9, or a king.

In this situation, you should not slowplay a set because your opponents will probably call if they have any piece of the board. Play the hand aggressively and take the pot down now.

Types of Opponents

If you're playing against an opponent who habitually bluffs when others don't bet, don't take that play away from him when you hit your set.

Let's say you have those pocket kings again, and the board comes K♥ 7♠ 2♣. Play coy and check to him. You can even check to him on every street and let him bluff all the way.

If you bet the flop, the bluffer will probably fold since it's highly unlikely that he has much of a hand. However, if you check, he might see that as an opportunity to bluff the hand through.

Conversely, if you're up against a player who will not bet with a drawing hand, there's no sense in trying to trap him. Bet your trips and hope that he has found a hand good enough to call you with.

Position

Your seat at the table is a big factor in determining how to play a flopped set. Let's say that you called a small raise in a five-way pot with 3-3. The flop comes K♠ 10♦ 3♥.

You're the first player to act. What should you do?

Check. It's quite likely that one of the other four players in the hand will bet such a flop. If no one bets, that's not so bad either. If the turn is an ace, for example, you'll be able to trap a player holding A-K for even more chips.

If you're in last position, however, everything changes. You'll be able to see what everyone does before it's your turn to act. There's no downside to the flop being checked around. If everyone does check to you, bet! With any luck, someone will think you're trying to steal the pot, and they'll raise you.

More chips for you!

41

Bluffing at Paired Flops

The texture of the flop is an extremely important factor in hold'em, especially when you're deciding whether to bluff at a pot. Paired flops are particularly tricky. When a pair comes out on the flop, you're in good bluffing position. If you actually have what you're representing—you've made a set—it's likely that your opponent will be drawing dead or has very few outs. Let's check out an example.

You raise with Q-Q and two players call. Then the flop comes J♦ J♠ 4♣. This is either an excellent flop for your hand, or it's a deathtrap. If you bet and an opponent raises, you'll be faced with the classic poker question: Does he have the jack, or is he bluffing?

With a strong hand such as pocket queens, you'd normally lean toward calling a raise on the flop and deferring your critical decision until later in the hand.

What about when you don't have a hand that strong?

Let's say that you bet the flop with A-K and an opponent raises. It would be difficult to justify a call in this situation. If your opponent doesn't think you have the jack, he might try to bluff you with a hand as weak as 8-9.

Now, let's put you in charge. Here's the setting: Two players limp into the pot and you're sitting in the big blind with J-8. The flop comes 3♣ 3♠ 5♦.

Bluffing from a blind position is an excellent way to pick up some chips. Despite the fact that you completely missed this flop, it can be a good opportunity to bluff, as it's also unlikely that either of them stayed in with a 3 in his hand.

It's important to remember this: To avoid becoming too predictable, you should occasionally bluff from the blind on paired flops, and sometimes bet the flop when you hit your trips. Mixing it up will earn your bets more respect and make it more believable that you could actually have a hand when you do bluff.

Most intermediate to advanced players understand that these bluffing opportunities often turn into a war. It comes down to who is willing to make the bigger bluff. I recently saw this concept illustrated in a hand played out on television.

Player A raised to $300 with Q♠ 9♥ offsuit and Player B called with the 9♣ 7♣. The flop came 10♠ 10♦ 5♣ and Player A bet $600.

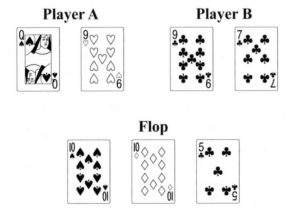

Player A   **Player B**

Flop

Apparently, Player B didn't believe that his opponent held a 10, so he raised it $1,000 more. Player A thought about it for a little while, and finally decided to reraise another $3,000.

This was an amazing read and a gutsy play. Player A made the bigger bluff, but the interesting thing is that, if Player B reraised all in, he would have won the pot. It was a stellar demonstration of poker at an elite level. Both players fought hard to win a pot with nothing-cards.

Of course, there should have been a warning at the bottom of the TV screen that read, "Do not try this at home!" Unless you have an excellent read of your opponent, these plays are a bit too risky.

Here's the bottom line: The key to bluffing at paired flops is making sure that you're mixing up your play. Just don't overdo it. Always keep your opponents guessing. If you fall into any pattern, bluffing or not, it won't take long for opponents to pick up on it. When that happens, you lose.

42

K-Q: A Dubious Hand

The one hand that beginning and intermediate players misplay more often than others is K-Q. The hand looks powerful—one that seemingly ranks right up there with A-K and A-Q—but it isn't in the same league as those premium cards. Novice players commonly overvalue the strength of K-Q when they flop a pair to it. Q-5-2 might look like an excellent flop for K-Q, but it can be very dangerous if an opponent has any of the following hands: 2-2, 5-5, Q-Q, A-Q, K-K or A-A.

An expert player is able to fold his K-Q on that flop if he senses that his opponent has a stronger hand. Most amateur players, however, just aren't sophisticated enough to know when to play the hand to the river and when to let it go.

An unimproved K-Q rarely holds up in a race to the river. Even a weak holding such as A-3 offsuit will beat it in the long run. If an ace hits, the K-Q is all but dead. If no king or queen hits, the A-3 wins by virtue of simply being higher.

Playing K-Q correctly is especially important in tournament poker when you're deciding whether to go all-in or to wait for a better situation.

If a tournament player goes all in before you, what hands could he have that would allow your K-Q to be in good shape? The only hands that K-Q dominates are K-J and K-10. It's much more likely that an all-in player has at least an ace, and oftentimes he'll have A-K or A-Q, which are both monster favorites over your cards. You'd have just three outs against either hand.

Now let's say that your opponent has a hand such as 10-10. Your K-Q still loses more than 55 percent of the time. See what I mean by dubious?

I strongly advise you to fold K-Q in the face of an early position raise. A raise from that spot represents a strong hand, one that usually dominates K-Q. However, K-Q is a good hand to attack the blinds with when you're the first player to enter the pot from middle or late position. In that situation, make a standard-size raise. If someone reraises, fold before you get yourself into trouble.

Suited cards usually don't make a world of difference, but with K-Q being suited, it is often enough of an added edge to allow you to call a raise in marginal situations. Here's why: You're hoping to flop a high pair or, better yet, to catch a straight or a high flush.

K-Q suited versus K-Q offsuit is a significantly better hand in a multiway pot. The more players that enter a pot, the stronger the average winning hand will be. In a heads-up pot the average winning hand may just be a high pair. But in a five-way action pot, you just might need that flush to win.

Now that you know these facts about K-Q, you can play the hand more reasonably. Yes, it'll score you some big pots, but don't get fooled into thinking that K-Q is a premium hand.

43

Playing Pocket Kings

The second best hand you can be dealt in Texas hold'em is K-K. But pocket cowboys can also become a scary proposition that can cost you a lot of money when they don't hold up. The trick to playing kings, or any big pocket pair, is to not fall in love with them.

In no-limit hold'em, it's almost never correct to throw away pocket kings before the flop. Yes, there are rare situations where that could be the right play, but I've been playing hold'em for a lot of years and have only folded kings preflop once. When I did, my opponent had pocket queens.

When you're dealt kings, you're going to play them. The only question is how. The standard answer is to simply bet them as you would any other strong hand: Come in for a moderate raise, about three times the size of the big blind. Just don't do anything that might raise suspicions.

Some believe you should make a larger raise to protect the hand. However, if you raise too much, you'll knock out all of your opponents and end up with just the blinds and the antes. That's not terrible, mind you, but A-A and K-K are hands that don't come along very often, and it's important to maximize your profit when they do. So raise, or even reraise, but don't make a play that your opponents may see as peculiar.

Let's say that you're heading to the flop. There's only one card that you'd absolutely hate to see and that's the ace—unless of course, there's a king sitting right next to it!

Sure enough, an ace comes on the flop. Now what? That doesn't mean you should immediately abort mission. Your opponent may not have an ace, which means that your kings are still ahead.

How to best proceed with your K-K depends on several factors: position, texture of the board, and your stack size.

Position

If you're out of position, it's usually best to check the kings and wait to see if your opponent bets the ace. If he does, you'll have to delve into your memory bank and ask yourself whether your opponent is much of a bluffer. Unless you feel very strongly that he's lying, dump the kings right on the flop.

On the other hand, if you have position, your opponent will likely check to you. In that case, you have two options: bet now and hope he folds, or check behind him protecting yourself from a possible check-raise.

When to bet and when to check is a function of the texture of the board.

Texture of the Board

If the flop comes A-6-6, A-A-7, or A-7-2, feel free to check your K-K. If your kings are indeed the best hand after the flop, they'll likely be the best hand by the river too. If you check it down to the river, you protect yourself from being bluffed. At the same time, you might even induce your opponent to attempt a bluff.

However, if the texture of the board is A♥ 8♠ 9♥, then you can take one stab at the flop to protect yourself against a drawing hand. If you're raised, though, you're pretty much forced to fold your kings. Why? Because if you're behind, only two cards remain in the deck that can save you.

Stack Size

If you're in a poker tournament and are low on chips at the flop, go all in with your pocket kings. If someone has an ace, that's just bad luck and there isn't much you can do about that.

However, if you're sitting on a big stack, proceed cautiously and dump the hand if the action gets heated.

I get tons of e-mail from people who tell me about their bad luck with pocket kings. While it's obviously unlucky to lose with cowboys, it's apparent to me that many of these players got married to the hand and lost more than they should have. You don't need to repeat their mistake!

44

Are Suited Cards Worth the Risk?

In a book I recently read, the author actually said that if he were playing a hand like 6-7 in a no-limit hold'em game, he'd prefer the hand be offsuit rather than the same suit. His thinking was that if he made a flush with a 6-7, it would be a small one, and he would risk losing a lot of money if his opponent hit a higher flush.

While that's true, it isn't enough of a negative to make unsuited cards more valuable than suited ones. In fact, starting out with suited cards has many more advantages above and beyond the low percentage of time that you'll actually complete your flush.

Let's look at an example. You're on the button and decide to limp into the pot with the 6♥ 7♥. Three other players are still in. The flop comes J♥ 8♦ 4♥. You need a 5 to fill the straight, or you can catch any heart to make a flush.

For the moment, let's say that your 6-7 is not suited. In that case, it would be difficult to call a post-flop bet with only four outs to make a straight. Also, with two hearts on the flop, even if you hit your 5, if it's the 5♥, you could lose to a flush.

Or, you might lose action if opponents fear that you have made the flush.

The biggest advantage about being suited, however, is the extra opportunity it affords you to semibluff after the flop. A semibluff is when you bet with a drawing hand hoping to steal the pot right away. Even when that doesn't work, you can still get lucky and make your hand.

Here's another scenario.

You   **Opponent**

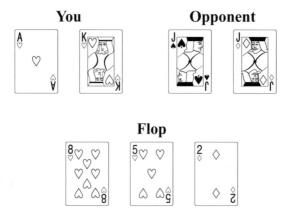

Flop

You're holding A♥ K♥ and the flop comes 8♥ 5♥ 2♦. You have a powerful hand despite the fact that you have no pair. If an opponent with a hand such as J♠ J♦ bets, you can raise him as a strong semibluff. Even if he calls, you're still the favorite to win the pot. You could hit one of nine remaining hearts, three aces, or three kings. That's a total of 15 outs with the turn and river cards still to come.

Let's get back to the fear of losing big pots with small, suited connectors. Yes, that's definitely something one should be concerned with, but here are three ways to minimize the damage when these situations arise.

- Proceed cautiously if all you have is a small flush draw with no pair or straight draw to go with it.

- Don't get involved in a big pot. Hitting your flush doesn't mean that you have to make a big bet.
- You don't have to bet at all if you're worried about an opponent having a bigger flush. Simply check on the river, and look to call his bet, provided it's not too large. If he bets big, and you suspect that you're beat, throw away your small flush.

To become a great poker player, you'll sometimes have to let go of strong hands. Sure, you'll occasionally be bluffed out of the pot, but if you never get bluffed at the poker table, you actually aren't playing all that well.

So, is it better to be suited?

Most definitely. It shouldn't be the deciding factor for playing a hand such as A-K, but it certainly should be a consideration when holding cards that are more marginal.

45

Playing Suited Connectors

Playing suited connectors from time to time makes you less predictable. When played sensibly, cards such as 6♥ 7♥ have the potential to make very strong hands—straights, flushes, and even full houses—that could result in a handsome payday. However, if you play these hands poorly after the flop, you risk losing your whole stack.

You shouldn't play suited connectors merely for the sake of playing them; you have to have a plan. Here are some guidelines that will help you take down some pots and avoid catastrophes.

Understand Your Goal

With a hand like 8♣ 9♣, you're hoping to hit a straight or a flush. Since your flush could be in bad shape against a higher flush, ideally you'd like to flop a straight, two pair, trips, or even a full house. Also, you should avoid overvaluing any hand when you simply flop one pair, even if it is the highest pair on the board.

Suppose the flop comes 9♠ 6♦ 4♥. You have a decent

hand, but not strong enough to play against any significant action. If you bet this flop and an opponent raises, consider folding immediately. There are few hands that you can beat, unless your opponent is bluffing.

If you suspect a bluff and decide to continue to the river, your goal should shift to manipulating the size of the pot. Keep it small. Trust me, you don't want to play a huge pot with just top pair and a weak kicker.

Don't Bet Yourself Out of a Hand

The traditional method of playing a flush draw on the flop is to bet it as a semibluff. Instead, consider checking the flop in the hope of getting a free card to complete your hand.

If you make the flush, and it's checked around to you, opponents may be less inclined to believe you made a hand, thus garnering you more action.

Betting a flush or straight draw in early position is less risky than doing so in late position. While you should be aggressive in late position, betting draws after the flop can actually cost you a bet if your hand doesn't improve. Even worse, someone could check-raise you an amount so large that you'll be forced to fold your good drawing hand.

Let's say there are five players in the pot and you're last to act. You hold a suited connector, one-gap hand: the J♣ 9♣. The flop comes Q♣ 8♠ 2♣, giving you a flush draw and an inside straight draw. Everyone checks to you. Making a bet here isn't a bad idea.

What happens, though, if you bet the flop and the small blind check-raises you all in?

He may have a hand like Q-8. You're way behind, and your earlier bet has cost you a free opportunity to hit your draw. I'm not saying that you can't ever bet your draws on the flop. Just be aware of the situation. Then use your reading skills to figure out if one of your opponents has a strong hand.

Bluffing at Missed Flops

If you're playing suited connectors solely on their payoff potential, then you're likely going to lose money. Betting only when you have a strong hand, or always checking when you miss, allows opponents to get an easy read on your playing style.

Suppose you raise from late position before the flop with small connectors such as the 4♣ 6♣. The flop comes A♦ 7♠ 2♥. Take a stab at the pot with a bet, especially since you're in position. Unless an opponent has an ace, he'll likely fold, fearing that your preflop raise represented an ace in the hole.

Playing Suited Connectors Out of Position

While suited connectors such as 5♥ 6♥ or 9♠ 10♠ have a lot of potential, you'll need to be careful that you don't bleed your stack to death by playing them in the wrong situations. So, when is the right time?

It's best to play these hands from late position rather than early position. Every hold'em poker book beats you over the head with constant reminders that position is power. Let me beat you with that reminder one more time!

Here are some strategies for playing suited connectors in position and out of position.

In a no-limit hold'em game, let's say that you call a small preflop raise in position with the 6♥ 7♥. The flop comes J♥ 9♠ 4♥. It's just you and the raiser. He checks. In this case, with position, you have two viable options: Check and take the free card, or bet in the hopes of winning the pot on a semi-bluff.

You'll often want to check, just in case your opponent is trying to trap you on the flop. If you do bet, your opponent may come over the top with a big raise, forcing you to fold your drawing hand.

What if your opponent bets the flop? Once again, you have options. You can fold if the bet is too big, you can call and hope to catch your flush, or you can raise as a semibluff.

The situation is reversed when you're out of position and your opponent acts last. Now, your options are much more limited.

Remember this rule: In order to make money with hands like 6♥ 7♥, you need to be able to control the pot size. You don't want to invest too much money before the flop, or too much after it, when you have a drawing hand.

When you're out of position, you're in exactly that tough spot: You have less control of the pot size. If you check on the flop, your opponent will bet if he has a strong hand. If you call on the flop, you've essentially handed control over to him. That's not a terrible idea, mind you, as you should always respect your opponent's power of position.

Still, checking and calling won't put you in a great situation. It will be difficult for you to win this pot with a bluff later in the hand. Basically, you're banking on making the flush.

On the flop, what if you check-raise instead? That'll work when your opponent is bluffing, but it will cost you a lot more money when he's holding the goods. It's a risky move that often works, but the cost is very high when it doesn't.

Suppose you bet the flop as a semibluff? That only makes the pot bigger. If your opponent likes the flop, he'll just raise an amount so big that you'll be forced to fold your drawing hand without ever getting to see the next card.

Okay, now let's review. In position, you have the luxury of being able to see more free cards, keep the pot small, and maintain control of the hand. That's extremely valuable leverage. Out of position, you have a lot more guesswork to do, and it's best to simply play it safe.

Clearly, it's easier to play suited connectors, or any hand for that matter, from late position. Occasionally, however, I recommend playing your suited connectors from early position so that you don't become too predictable. When you do venture in, play cautiously—and always remember that position is king and must be respected at all times.

Think of suited connectors in baseball terms. Straights and flushes are home runs when they hit the flop. But when you don't knock it out of the park, just make it to first base—and then try to steal a base or two!

46

Limping In with Pocket Aces

There are opposing schools of thought as to whether you should limp in before the flop when holding a big pocket pair like A-A in no-limit Texas hold'em. Some players believe that it's a mistake to give your opponents the opportunity to outdraw you for free. This school advises you to raise preflop to narrow down the field when you're dealt A-A in order to increase your odds of winning the pot.

That betting strategy makes some sense. While it's true that pocket aces will win a high percentage of the time against a single opponent, with seven or eight players sticking around to see the flop, the chances of your aces winning the pot go way down.

The opposing school of thought is that raising too much with your pocket rockets will result in folds around the table. Your monster hand will end up winning just the blinds. Now, that's not a terrible result—but when you're dealt a powerful hand like A-A, you definitely want some action on the hand. Ideally, another player will raise you back, and then you can go all in before the flop.

The theory behind limping in with A-A is that you'll be able to trap one of your opponents for more of their chips. Your smooth call before the flop may be perceived as a sign of weakness. A player with a hand such as 9-9 or A-Q might decide to attack and raise. When that happens, you can spring into action and reraise the bet again.

Which strategy works the best?

As is the case in most poker situations, there are merits to both plays. Words like "never" and "always" don't often apply to poker. If you tell your opponents that you never limp in with aces, you're guilty of thinking, and playing, inside the box.

As a general rule, when you're dealt A-A, make a small raise before the flop. However, depending upon the situation, limping in may work best, and will definitely add deception to your game.

Limping in with aces to trap your opponents works best when you're at a table with very aggressive players. The problem is that if no one else raises before the flop, you'll find yourself in a multiway pot. Should that be the case, it's critical that you don't get married to your hand after the flop. That's often a problem for novice players.

If you decide to set a trap by limping in and the plan fails, you must have the discipline to play the hand cautiously after the flop. If you don't trust yourself, then limping in with pocket bullets isn't for you.

Yet, if you never limp in with aces, you might as well put a target on your forehead when you do limp into a pot. It will become apparent to your opponents that when you limp in before the flop, you probably don't have a big pair. That's revealing too much information. You'd be playing too predictably.

If you ever want to limp in with hands such as 5-6 suited or pocket fours and hope to see the flop without a raise, you must add "limping in strong" to your repertoire of ploys.

You don't have to do it often. If you have limped in strong

even once, observant opponents will notice and will be wary of your future limps. In a sense, the occasional limp with a very strong hand will protect you from being attacked. Aggressive players will be less likely to pounce on you when you just call if they know that you sandbag from time to time.

With A-A, first consider the situation. Then make either a small raise or limp in; either strategy can be correct. Though limping in with A-A isn't necessarily the best way to play the hand, doing it from time to time will free you up to be more creative and allow you to see some cheaper flops with marginal hands.

Another strategy you can use to mix up your play with A-A is smooth calling. We'll take a closer look at that play coming up next.

47

Setting a Trap by Smooth Calling with Pocket Aces

To win a really big pot in a game of no-limit Texas hold'em, you'll often have to set a trap for your opponents, especially if they are good players. That's because most solid players won't go broke in a typical hand unless they either have a strong hand themselves, or you've done a good job of fooling them.

In the previous section, we discussed limping in with A-A before the flop to add deception to your game. Now let's look at how you can set traps before the flop with A-A, using an effective play known as smooth calling.

Smooth calling describes a strategy in which a player just calls an opponent's raise rather than reraising it. By smooth calling with your pocket aces, you conceal the strength of your hand, which often turns into extra bets later. Check out these situations.

You and two other players are in the hand. The opponent to your right raises before the flop, you smooth call with A-A, and the last player makes an aggressive reraise. He'll figure that since you just smooth called the initial raise, he has you beat and only has to worry about the other guy.

He's wrong. When the action gets back to you, pounce on him with a big reraise.

You can also trap a strong opponent after the flop. Let's say that the flop comes K-7-3, and your opponent holds K-Q. He bets into you. You can safely smooth call here. Chances are that your aces are going to beat him for a big pot since he'll believe that he has the best hand.

Another key benefit to smooth calling with A-A is that it will trap opponents who otherwise wouldn't lose a penny.

Let's say that a player raises and you don't smooth call. Instead, you reraise with your aces. If someone behind you picks up A-K, he'll probably fold his hand in the face of the two raises. If he doesn't, he's a bad player and will probably be broke soon enough anyway.

When you smooth call, however, any player with A-K is going to call one raise before the flop. Then, if you're lucky enough to hit a flop like A-7-2 or K-8-3, your opponent will be completely trapped in the hand. In both cases, he'll think that his hand is strong enough to play for all his chips. You'll have him all but dead.

Once your opponents catch on to the fact that you sometimes smooth call with aces, you'll benefit in other ways as well. For example, suppose that later in the game, you decide to smooth call a raise with small suited connectors such as the 5♠ 6♠ in the hope of seeing the flop cheaply. A player may show you newfound respect and just call with a hand that he normally would reraise with.

The beauty of smooth calling is that even when people know that you use this play, they have little defense against it. In fact, if your opponents believe that you smooth call regularly, bluffing opportunities will open up for you when the flop comes ragged. They have seen you smooth call with A-A once, and that picture will stick in their minds for a long time, even though you may not do it again the entire session.

I must warn you, though, that there are real dangers in slowplaying A-A preflop. Allow players to affordably chase and they'll sometimes catch you. That's poker. Don't focus on how often you win with pocket aces, but rather on how much money you win when you do.

When you get to a flop with aces after a smooth call, proceed with a bit of caution. If the flop comes J-J-4, there's no reason to get too frisky. If your opponent has trips, you're obviously cooked. The last thing you want to do is set a trap with aces and then go broke with them.

When the board gets scary, play your pocket aces with care.

48

When A-K Misses the Flop

Though not as good-looking as pocket aces, A-K is a pretty starter. Just remember that, as attractive as it appears, it's still a drawing hand. It's a drawing hand because it won't even beat a lowly pair of deuces without improving! If you don't hit an ace or king on the flop, you'll often be forced to dump Big Slick.

One of the biggest mistakes amateurs make when playing A-K is that they continue to chase after the flop if the hand doesn't improve. If you don't catch a piece of the flop, don't invest another penny in the pot.

Here are some other important factors to consider when you're dealt Big Slick.

Number of Opponents

The more players in a pot, the more likely that your unimproved A-K is behind. In fact, you could easily be drawing dead.

Let's say that you raise with the A♣ K♠ and four other players call. The flop comes 9♥ 6♦ 7♦.

It's highly likely that one of your opponents has at least

a pair, and someone could even have a set or a straight. Even if you catch an ace and a king, you're still highly likely to lose the pot.

Don't bluff at this flop. I'll say it again: A bet saved is just as good as a bet earned.

Position

If your A-K misses the flop, and your opponent has position, you'll just have to respect his power of position and proceed cautiously. If he bets at you—even though he might be bluffing—you simply don't have a strong enough hand to justify a call.

However, if you're the player in late position with an unimproved A-K, then you can call on the flop, whether you miss or not. Your call may freeze your opponent, which might allow you to pick up the pot on the turn with a bet. Whether you improve on the turn is irrelevant because you're playing your opponent, not your cards.

Added Outs

You'll often miss your A-K and not make a pair. But there's still hope. You may find yourself with new added outs that give you a straight or a flush draw. If you're in this situation and only face a small bet, it might be worth calling to see one more card, especially if you're drawing to the nuts.

Keep in mind, however that a four-flush with A-K on the flop is a powerful hand that should be played aggressively, but a gutshot straight draw on a flop like Q-10-4 must be played cautiously.

Type of Opponent

Studying your opponents will help you make better A-K decisions. For example, if your opponent is a mad bluffer, you should be more inclined to look him up by calling his bet. But if you're facing a tight opponent who only plays high cards, don't even think about calling his bet if the flop comes something like Q-9-8.

Board Texture

Once you're able to put competitors on a range of hands, you'll have a better feel for the types of flops that will miss them. Not surprisingly, these same flops are also good for your A-K.

Let's say that you raise before the flop with A-K and a tight player calls. If the flop is 2-2-4, rest assured that he doesn't have any piece of that board. Go ahead and bet your A-K to protect it, while at the same time representing a big pair. If your opponent doesn't have a pocket pair (and even if he has a 4), he'll likely fold after your bet.

49

Why Professionals Hate to Play A-Q

Ask professional poker players which hole cards cause them the most difficulty and I would bet that more than half will say A-Q. Ace-queen is a powerful starter, but the problem is that it matches up poorly against other premium hands. Any player, even a pro, must tread carefully when dealt an A-Q.

If an opponent has A-A, K-K, Q-Q, or even A-K, your chances of winning with A-Q are slim. That's not the only problem with this hand. Unlike terrible starters such as 7-2, which are easy to fold, an A-Q is simply too powerful to fold before the flop for a minimal bet.

Since you are going to play A-Q most of the time, there are some rules to follow that will make playing this tricky hand easier. Here's the first rule of thumb: When facing an all-in reraise before the flop, A-Q is usually in horrible shape and, in most cases, should be folded.

Only call an all-in bet with A-Q when you're getting pot odds of more than 2 to 1, or when you think your opponent's range of hands may include middle pairs such as 9-9, 10-10, or J-J. Against those hands, A-Q matches up just fine as only a small underdog.

You should not be tempted to call an all-in bet with A-Q. The only time you'd be a favorite is against hands such as A-J or K-Q. An opponent who reraises all in before the flop—unless he's a loose maniac—will usually have A-Q dominated.

It's facing those premium hands that will get you in deep trouble as more than a 3 to 1 underdog to win the hand.

Before the flop, if no one has raised, you should absolutely raise with A-Q. Your objective is to win the blinds and antes, or play heads-up against one opponent. Hopefully, that player will be the big blind and you'll have position throughout the hand.

However, if someone raises from early position, you must strongly consider folding. A-Q isn't a good calling hand. Unless you're leading the betting, you'll be on the defensive and in trouble for the rest of the hand.

Now let's say that you've made it to the flop. There aren't many flops that can be considered safe for A-Q. Because of this, you must play cautiously. Taking a stab at the flop, whether you hit your hand or not, is an acceptable play, but if there is any resistance at all, you must abort the mission and fold.

The trickiest part about playing A-Q is when you catch an ace on the flop. Suppose the flop comes A♣ 7♦ 3♠. A-Q looks like a very powerful hand, trailing only A-K, two pair, or trips.

Although those hands are unlikely, when an opponent does hit one, you're doomed if you don't proceed carefully. Ask yourself this question: "What kind of hand could my opponent have in order to play a big pot in this situation?"

I'll tell you this much: If you play a big pot with A-Q on that A-7-3 flop against a pro, I guarantee that you're in terrible shape. If he decides to put all of his chips into the pot, he'll likely show you a hand such as A♠ 7♠, or maybe even pocket sevens.

Here are a few more tips that should make playing A-Q a little easier.

Don't Call Early Position Raises

We discussed how to play A-Q against an all-in bet, but how should you play this tricky hand against a simple raise? Against an early position raise, A-Q isn't the kind of hand you want to call with. In fact, you'd be much better off with 6♥ 7♥ than the A♣ Q♠.

Why? An early position raise usually signifies strength, which means that your A-Q will be dominated against any of the following hands: A-A, K-K, Q-Q, or A-K.

You want to be the preflop aggressor with A-Q. Don't be a caller.

Play Cautiously After the Flop

When you do play A-Q, remember that unless the flop comes something like A-Q-4 or K-J-10, your hand will always be vulnerable. Let's say that the flop comes Q-10-8. Don't get so excited about playing a big pot here. In fact, if an opponent raises in this situation, you should seriously consider folding.

Why would you fold top pair with top kicker?

Because you can't beat any of the following hands: J-9, 8-8, 10-10, Q-Q, Q-10, 10-8, K-K, or A-A. Even if your hand leads preflop, chances are that other players will have several outs to beat you. The A-Q would even be vulnerable to a hand like J-10 should a 9, 10, or jack arrive on the turn or river.

Holding A-Q, your goal should be to win the pot immediately on the flop. If you don't, play cautiously and don't allow yourself to lose more chips than you need to.

Play Aggressively From the Blinds

Playing A-Q out of position after the flop is no picnic. It's hard to win the pot if you don't catch a pair on the flop unless you plan to make a big, risky bluff, which is not a bad strategy when playing against a conservative, early-position raiser.

However, when you're facing a loose player's raise, it's

better to simply call and then proceed carefully. Now, if that raise comes from the same aggressive player, but he's sitting in middle to late position, it makes more sense to try to win the pot before the flop.

Now, let's look at a hand. A frisky player has made it $600 to go before the flop. The blinds are at $100/$200 with a $25 ante. It comes back to you in the big blind holding A-Q, and it's $400 more to call. Against a skilled player, put the pressure back on him with a big reraise.

How much?

A reraise of $1,800 isn't enough to scare him off. Lean toward a raise of $2,500 to $3,000. This will quickly define your opponent's hand. If he folds, he obviously had a marginal hand, and was just trying to steal the blinds. If he reraises, though, your A-Q is dead meat. Fold the hand.

Your difficult decision comes when he just calls your raise. His most likely hands would be 9-9, 10-10, J-J, K-K, or A-K. You must play very carefully from there on in.

But remember one more thing. If an opponent calls your reraise, don't automatically make a continuation bet after the flop. Respect his call and understand that he probably has the better hand. This is no time to get reckless and melt away your stack with what very well could be the second-best hand.

50

Two Trouble Hands that Might Come in Second

Q-9 and J-8 aren't exactly monsters. In fact, these two hands should come with a warning label because they could cost you all of your chips. I'm referring to situations where you end up making a straight but you lose to a higher straight.

Let's say the flop comes 10-J-K. You obviously have a strong hand with Q-9, but it's a loser if an opponent holds A-Q.

J-8 gets into trouble when the board comes 9-10-Q. In this situation, someone playing a K-J makes the higher straight. You'll lose here, too, unless you're able to make an excellent read.

Potential second-best straights are always dangerous hands to play. In particular, Q-9 and J-8 are more susceptible to finishing second best. Why? The hands that most players will pay to see the flop with are precisely the ones that will beat you.

Lower cards give you less to worry about. For example, suppose you play 6-3. The flop comes 4-5-7. While it's certainly possible that an opponent could be holding the dreaded 8-6, it's much less likely since players typically prefer to play high cards and fold lower ones.

As a rule, avoid playing the Q-9 and the J-8 against a raise. Calling a raise with either of these hands will cost you in the long run, especially if the raiser is in early position.

Let's look at a situation where someone raises in front of you. Suppose a player raises in first position and you call with Q-9. The flop comes K-J-10, and your opponent bets the pot. This puts you in a very difficult situation. It's difficult to know for sure whether he has an A-Q, or a pocket pair such as A-A, K-K, J-J, or 10-10. You're in good shape against any pocket pair; most players holding Q-9 would raise in this spot.

But raising could present another problem: What if your opponent reraises? It's starting to look as though he has A-Q, but he might very well make that move with three of a kind. Folding against trips would be a huge mistake, but putting all of your money in against A-Q would be an even bigger blunder.

You can see why I'm not a fan of either of these two hands.

That reminds me, I'm also leery about playing a hand such as K♠ 4♠. The king is a strong card but the 4 kicker is pitiful. When you catch a king on the flop, you'll still be worried about someone having a better kicker. That's not even the worst part about K-x suited hands. If you're actually lucky enough to catch a flush, it'll often end up being second-best.

It's common to see a king-high flush lose to the ace-high flush since people usually play hands such as A♠ 10♠. Unless you're the Amazing Kreskin, or you possess incredible hand-reading skills, it's going to be difficult to get away from second-best flushes without losing a big pot.

Here's a note specific to tournament play.

You need to play a lot of hands in order to succeed in no-limit hold'em tournaments, and hands like Q-9 and J-8 can fit that bill. In tournaments, go ahead and play these hands, with this warning: Be prepared to put the brakes on if you find yourself looking at a flop that could make your hand second-best.

FINAL THOUGHTS

In the conclusion to my first "Wisdom" book, I suggested that you think outside the box. This time around, I've given you some ways to stretch the envelope in no-limit and limit hold'em tournaments and cash games.

I've never been an advocate of playing the game the same way every time you sit down at the table. Players will know the kinds of hands you play and how you play them, which is not a profitable approach. If you've seen me play on TV, you know that my unpredictable style makes my play hard to read. I end up winning pots with weak hands by effectively bluffing out confused opponents and maximizing other pots when I have good hands, but my opponent doesn't believe me. I keep dancing and the other players keep paying for the music.

But that doesn't mean I don't rely on solid hold'em fundamentals as the core of successful approach. I do. Every winner does, and I've tried to impart that knowledge in this book.

I implore you to use this knowledge wisely and perhaps we'll meet over a big hand at a final table with you congratulating me on the victory—or perhaps the other way around!

GREAT CARDOZA POKER BOOKS
ADD THESE TO YOUR LIBRARY - ORDER NOW!

DANIEL NEGREANU'S POWER HOLD'EM STRATEGY *by Daniel Negreanu.* This power-packed book on beating no-limit hold'em is one of the three most influential poker books ever written. Negreanu headlines a collection of young great players—Todd Brunson, David Williams. Erick Lindgren, Evelyn Ng and Paul Wasicka—who share their insider professional moves and winning secrets. You'll learn about short-handed and heads-up play, high-limit cash games, a powerful beginner's strategy to neutralize professional players, and how to mix up your play and bluff and win big pots. The centerpiece, however, is Negreanu's powerful and revolutionary small ball strategy. You'll learn how to play hold'em with cards you never would have played before—and with fantastic results. The preflop, flop, turn and river will never look the same again. A must-have! 520 pages, $34.95.

HOLD'EM WISDOM FOR ALL PLAYERS *By Daniel Negreanu.* Superstar poker player Daniel Negreanu provides 50 easy-to-read and right-to-the-point hold'em strategy nuggets that will immediately make you a better player at cash games and tournaments. His wit and wisdom makes for great reading; even better, it makes for killer winning advice. Conversational, straightforward, and educational, this book covers topics as diverse as the top 10 rookie mistakes to bullying bullies and exploiting your table image. 176 pages, $14.95.

POKER WIZARDS *by Warwick Dunnett.* In the tradition of Super System, an exclusive collection of champions and superstars have been brought together to share their strategies, insights, and tactics for winning big money at poker, specifically no-limit hold'em tournaments. This is priceless advice from players who individually have each made millions of dollars in tournaments, and collectively, have won more than 20 WSOP bracelets, two WSOP main events, 100 major tournaments and $50 million in tournament winnings! Featuring Daniel Negreanu, Dan Harrington, Marcel Luske, Kathy Liebert, Mike Sexton, Mel Judah, Marc Salem, T.J. Cloutier and Chris "Jesus" Ferguson. This must-read book is a goldmine for serious players, aspiring pros, and future champions! 352 pgs, $19.95.

MILLION DOLLAR HOLD'EM: Winning Big in Limit Cash Games *by Johnny Chan and Mark Karowe.* Learn how to win money consistently at limit hold'em, poker's most popular cash game, from one of poker's living legends. You'll get a rare opportunity to get into the mind of the man who has won ten World Series of Poker titles—tied for the most ever with Doyle Brunson—as Johnny picks out illustrative hands and shows how he thinks his way through the betting and the bluffing. No book so thoroughly details the thought process of how a hand is played, the alternative ways it could have been played, and the best way to win session after session. *Essential* reading for cash players. 400 pages, $29.95.

TOURNAMENT TIPS FROM THE POKER PROS *by Shane Smith.* Essential advice from poker theorists, authors, and tournament winners on the best strategies for winning the big prizes at low-limit rebuy tournaments. Learn proven strategies for each of the four stages of play—opening, middle, late and final—how to avoid 26 potential traps, advice on rebuys, aggressive play, clock-watching, inside moves, top 20 tips for winning tournaments, more. Advice from Brunson, McEvoy, Cloutier, Caro, Malmuth, others. 160 pages, $14.95.

NO-LIMIT TEXAS HOLD'EM: The New Player's Guide to Winning Poker's Biggest Game *by Brad Daugherty & Tom McEvoy.* For experienced limit players who want to play no-limit or rookies who has never played before, two world champions show readers how to evaluate the strength of a hand, determine the amount to bet, understand opponents' play, plus how to bluff and when to do it. Seventy-four game scenarios, unique betting charts for tournament play, and sections on essential principles and strategies show you how to get to the winner's circle. Special section on beating online tournaments. 288 pages, $19.95.

GREAT CARDOZA POKER BOOKS
ADD THESE TO YOUR LIBRARY - ORDER NOW!

SUPER SYSTEM by Doyle Brunson. This classic book is considered by the pros to be the best book ever written on poker! Jam-packed with advanced strategies, theories, tactics and money-making techniques, no serious poker player can afford to be without this hard-hitting information. Includes fifty pages of the most precise poker statistics ever published. Features chapters written by poker's biggest superstars, such as Dave Sklansky, Mike Caro, Chip Reese, Joey Hawthorne, Bobby Baldwin, and Doyle. Essential strategies, advanced play, and no-nonsense winning advice on making money at 7-card stud (razz, high-low split, cards speak, and declare), draw poker, lowball, and hold'em (limit and no-limit).This is a must-read for any serious poker player. 628 pages, $29.95.

SUPER SYSTEM 2 by Doyle Brunson. The most anticipated poker book ever, SS2 expands upon the original with more games and professional secrets from the best in the world. Superstar contributors include Daniel Negreanu, winner of multiple WSOP gold bracelets and 2004 Poker Player of the Year; Lyle Berman, 3-time WSOP gold bracelet winner, founder of the World Poker Tour, and super-high stakes cash player; Bobby Baldwin, 1978 World Champion; Johnny Chan, 2-time World Champion and 10-time WSOP bracelet winner; Mike Caro, poker's greatest researcher, theorist, and instructor; Jennifer Harman, the world's top female player and one of ten best overall; Todd Brunson, winner of more than 20 tournaments; and Crandell Addington, no-limit hold'em legend. 672 pgs, $29.95.

CARO'S GUIDE TO DOYLE BRUNSON'S SUPER SYSTEM by Mike Caro. Working with World Champion Doyle Brunson, the legendary Mike Caro has created a fresh look to the "Bible" of all poker books, adding new and personal insights that help you understand the original work. Caro breaks 36 concepts into either "Analysis, Commentary, Concept, Mission, Play-By-Play, Psychology, Statistics, Story, or Strategy. Lots of illustrations and winning concepts give even more value to this great work. 86 pages, 8 1/2 x 11, $19.95.

MY 50 MOST MEMORABLE HANDS by Doyle Brunson. Great players, legends, and poker's most momentous events march in and out of fifty years of unforgettable hands. Sit side-by-side with Doyle as he replays the excitement and life-changing moments of the most thrilling and crucial hands in the history of poker: from his early games as a rounder in the rough-and-tumble "Wild West" years—where a man was more likely to get shot as he was to get a straight flush—to the nail-biting excitement of his two world championship titles. Relive million dollar hands and the high stakes tension of sidestepping police, hijackers and murderers. A thrilling collection of stories and sage poker advice. 168 pages, $14.95.

THE POKER TOURNAMENT FORMULA by Arnold Snyder. Start making money now in fast no-limit hold'em tournaments with these radical and never-before-published concepts and secrets for beating tournaments. You'll learn why cards don't matter as much as the dynamics of a tournament—your position, the size of your chip stack, who your opponents are, and above all, the structure. Poker tournaments offer one of the richest opportunities to come along in decades. Every so often, a book comes along that changes the way players attack a game and provides them with a big advantage over opponents. Gambling legend Arnold Snyder has written such a book. 368 pages, $19.95.

POKER TOURNAMENT FORMULA 2: Advanced Strategies for Big Money Tournaments by Arnold Snyder. Probably the greatest tournament poker book ever written, and the most controversial in the last decade, Snyder's revolutionary work debunks commonly (and falsely) held beliefs. Snyder reveals the power of chip utility—the real secret behind winning tournaments—and covers utility ranks, tournament structures, small- and long-ball strategies, patience factors, the impact of structures, crushing the Harringbots and other player types, tournament phases, and much more. Includes big sections on Tools, Strategies, and Tournament Phases. A must buy! 496 pages, $24.95.

GREAT CARDOZA POKER BOOKS
ADD THESE TO YOUR LIBRARY - ORDER NOW!

CARO'S MOST PROFITABLE HOLD'EM ADVICE *by Mike Caro.* When Mike Caro writes a book on winning, all poker players take notice. And they should: The "Mad Genius of Poker" has influenced just about every professional player and world champion alive. You'll journey far beyond the traditional tactical tools offered in most poker books and for the first time, have access to the entire missing arsenal of strategies left out of everything you've ever seen or experienced. Caro's first major work in two decades is packed with hundreds of powerful ideas, concepts, and strategies, many of which will be new to you—they have never been made available to the general public. This book represents Caro's lifelong research into beating the game of hold em. 408 pages, $24.95

CARO'S BOOK OF POKER TELLS *by Mike Caro.* One of the ten greatest books written on poker, this must-have book should be in every player's library. If you're serious about winning, you'll realize that most of the profit comes from being able to read your opponents. Caro reveals the the secrets of interpreting *tells*—physical reactions that reveal information about a player's cards—such as shrugs, sighs, shaky hands, eye contact, and many more. Learn when opponents are bluffing, when they aren't and why—based solely on their mannerisms. Over 170 photos of players in action and play-by-play examples show the actual tells. These powerful ideas will give you the decisive edge. 320 pages, $24.95.

HOW TO BEAT SIT-AND-GO POKER TOURNAMENTS by Neil Timothy. There is a lot of dead money up for grabs in the lower limit sit-and-gos and Neil Timothy shows you how to go and get it. The author, a professional player, shows you how to reach the last six places of lower limit sit-and-go tournaments four out of five times and then how to get in the money 25-35 percent of the time using his powerful, proven strategies. This book can turn a losing sit-and-go player into a winner, and a winner into a bigger winner. Also effective for the early and middle stages of one-table satellites.176 pages, $14.95.

CHAMPIONSHIP NO-LIMIT & POT-LIMIT HOLD'EM *by T. J. Cloutier & Tom McEvoy.* The bible for winning pot-limit and no-limit hold'em tournaments gives you all the answers to your most important questions: How do you get inside your opponents' heads and learn how to beat them at their own game? How can you tell how much to bet, raise, and reraise in no-limit hold'em? When can you bluff? How do you set up your opponents in pot-limit hold'em so that you can win a monster pot? What are the best strategies for winning no-limit and pot-limit tournaments, satellites, and supersatellites? Inspired advice you can bank on from two of the most recognizable figures in poker. 304 pages, $19.95.

CHAMPIONSHIP HOLD'EM *by T. J. Cloutier & Tom McEvoy.* Hard-hitting hold'em the way it's played *today* in both limit cash games and tournaments. Get killer advice on how to win more money in rammin'-jammin' games, kill-pot, jackpot, shorthanded, and full table cash games. You'll learn the thinking process for preflop, flop, turn, and river play with specific suggestions for what to do when good or bad things happen. Includes play-by-play analyses, advice on how to maximize profits against rocks in tight games, weaklings in loose games, experts in solid games, plus tournament strategies for small buy-in, big buy-in, rebuy, add-on, satellite and major tournaments. Wow! 392 pages, $19.95.

CHAMPIONSHIP OMAHA (Omaha High-Low, Pot-limit Omaha, Limit High Omaha) *by Tom McEvoy & T.J. Cloutier.* Clearly-written strategies and powerful advice from Cloutier and McEvoy who have won four World Series of Poker Omaha titles. You'll learn how to beat low-limit and high-stakes games, play against loose and tight opponents, and the differing strategies for rebuy and freezeout tournaments. Learn the best starting hands, when slowplaying a big hand is dangerous, what danglers are (and why winners don't play them), why you sometimes fold the nuts on the flop and would be correct in doing so, and overall, how you can win a lot of money at Omaha! 296 pages, illustrations, $19.95.

Order now at 1-800-577-WINS or go online to: www.cardozabooks.com